Fabulous&**Flirty** Felt

QUARRY

Fabulous & Flirty

Felt

GLOUCESTER MASSACHUSETTS

QUARRY BOOKS

**Stylish Handbag
and Accessory Patterns
to Knit and Felt**

Darlene Bruce

First published in the United States of America by Quarry Books,
a member of Quayside Publishing Group
33 Commercial Street
Gloucester, Massachusetts 01930-5089
Telephone: (978) 282-9590
Fax: (978) 283-2742
www.quarrybooks.com

Library of Congress Cataloging-in-Publication Data
Bruce, Darlene.
  Fabulous and flirty felt: stylish handbag and accessory patterns to knit and felt/ Darlene Bruce.
    p. cm.
  ISBN 1-59253-312-4 (pbk.)
  1. Knitting—Patterns. 2. Felting. 3. Handbags. 4. House furnishings. I. Title.
TT825.B783 2007
  746.43'20431—dc22   2006026830
                                                        CIP

ISBN-13: 978-1-59253-312-1
ISBN-10: 1-59253-312-4

10 9 8 7 6 5 4 3 2 1

Design: Todd Fairchild
Photography: Allan Penn
Technical Editing: Dorothy T. Ratigan
Shown on title page: Sassy Square Bags, pages 37–43; Felted Flower Pins, pages 79–81

Printed in China

To Violet, my sweet little kitty.
You will always be in my heart.

Contents

Introduction

As the interest in knitting has grown, knitters are looking for quick and easy projects. And knitting to felt is perfect for the beginner as well as the seasoned knitter. This book outlines the basics of knitting and crocheting, along with instructions for felting and yarn dyeing. Ten introductory projects from bags and accessories to home decor are included, plus numerous fun variations. There are also tips on how to make every project your own unique creation using custom-dyed yarns and creative knitted and crocheted trims.

Felting is simple and enjoyable as long as a few simple guidelines are followed. The section on felting outlines the basic method as well as tips and secrets on how to produce a beautifully proportioned felted item. There are also suggestions on yarn selection. A section on yarn dyeing opens up a whole world of customization, enabling your knitted and felted items to be one-of-a-kind pieces of fiber art. Yarn dyeing is economical and simple to do with a few tools from the kitchen, allowing you to create hand-dyed items without the hand-dyed price.

A beginning knitter can make most of the projects in this book; however, intermediate and advanced knitters will also find the techniques challenging and the construction and designs interesting. The book begins with four basic purse patterns, from evening to everyday styles, each with unique styling variations. Next, knitted and crocheted felted flower accessories will dress up any bag, coat, or hat. Flirty felted belts look great with jeans or used to cinch a flowing blouse or dress. Home decor projects round out the pattern section, with place mats, coasters, napkin rings, decorative rugs, and cute one-of-a-kind small beds for your favorite feline or canine friends.

I hope you enjoy making many of the projects in this book. The possibilities are endless when you have a few basic patterns to spark your creativity. Feel free to experiment and make each piece your own. Be forewarned; you may elicit quite a bit of attention with your fabulous felted bags and accessories as you walk down the street. If someone asks, you can proudly say that you created it yourself, and it was fun and easy to do. At least that is my hope in creating this book. So relax and enter the fabulous world of felted knits. Enjoy!

—Darlene

Basic Techniques

❀ If you are new to knitting and crocheting or if you haven't picked up needles and yarn in a while, this section provides a refresher course for basic stitches needed to make the projects in this book. Four foundation techniques are used to knit, including cast on, knit, purl, and bind off. Basic crocheting instructions, such as slip stitch, chain, and single crochet, are also included. Everyone has a unique style of knitting and crocheting, so feel free to do what works best for you. A stitch glossary is also provided, along with common abbreviations used in knitting and crochet.

If you haven't done any felting, then you will probably want to check out the section on felting techniques. It contains suggestions for yarns and tips for felting in your washing machine. The final section is on yarn dyeing with acid dyes or unsweetened powdered drink mixes. Complete dyeing instructions have been provided for creating fantastic tinted yarns using either dye method.

Knitting Basics

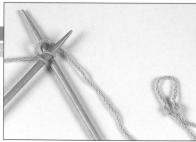

Fig 1.0

Casting On

There are many ways to cast on stitches for knitting. One versatile method is the cable cast-on. Form a slipknot and place it on a knitting needle (Fig 1.0). Hold the needle with the slipknot in your left hand. With your right hand, slip a second needle through the first loop and pull the yarn through, making a second loop. Place the second loop back on the left needle. You now have two stitches. Continue to add on stitches by drawing the yarn through the last loop on the needle until you have the desired number of stitches (Fig 1.1).

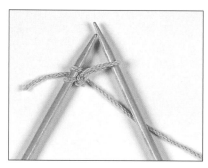

Fig 1.1

Knitting

Once you have cast on, then you can start knitting. Hold the needle with the cast-on stitches in your left hand. Hold the empty needle in your right hand. Insert the right needle (pointing it front to back) into the front of the first stitch on the left needle and wrap the yarn around the point of the right needle (Fig 1.2). Using the right needle, pull the yarn through the first stitch and off the left needle (Fig 1.3). You will now have one completed knit stitch on the right needle. Continue in this manner until all of the stitches on the left needle have been knit and you are at the end of the row.

Fig 1.2

Purling

The purl stitch is the reverse of the knit stitch. Hold the needle with the stitches in your left hand. Hold the empty needle in your right hand. Insert the right needle (pointing it back to front) into the front of the first stitch on the left needle and wrap the yarn around the point of the right

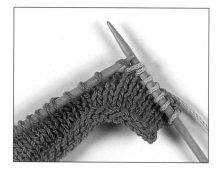

Fig 1.3

needle (Fig 1.4). Using the right needle, pull the yarn back through the first stitch and off the left needle (Fig 1.5). You will have one completed purl stitch on the right needle. Continue in this manner until all of the stitches on the left needle have been purled and you are at the end of the row.

Binding Off

This technique is used to finish your knitted piece and prevent the stitches from unraveling. Knit or purl the first two stitches. Using the left needle, pass the first stitch over the second stitch and completely off the point of the right needle (Fig 1.6). Knit or purl the next stitch and repeat, passing the previous stitch over the next stitch, until one stitch remains (Fig 1.7). Cut the yarn, leaving a tail; thread this tail into a tapestry needle and then through the last stitch. Pull to fasten the yarn off.

Gauge

The knitting gauge is the number of stitches and rows per inch. Factors that influence knitting gauge are needle size and yarn weight. Gauge determines the size of your final knitted piece. It is important to have the correct gauge even when knitting to felt. If your knitting gauge is too tight then there is no room to compact the felted fabric. To check gauge, knit a test swatch that is at least 4" (10 cm) square. Measure the swatch using a ruler or gauge tool. If the number of stitches and rows does not match the gauge specified in the pattern, you can change the needle size. To get more stitches per inch or a tighter knit, then use a smaller needle size. To get fewer stitches per inch or a looser knit, use a larger needle size.

Fig 1.4

Fig 1.5

Fig 1.6

Fig 1.7

Glossary

Backward Loop Cast-On

This is a very simple method for casting on. Make a backward loop as shown and place it on the needle in a backward position so that it doesn't unwind (Fig 2.0). Repeat for as many stitches as needed.

Fig 2.0

Knit Tube

I-cords are small knit tubes made by using two double-pointed needles. Cast on the number of stitches specified in a pattern using one double-pointed needle. Without turning the needle, slide the stitches to the opposite end. Pull the yarn around back to the needle tip and, with the second needle, knit the stitches (Fig. 2.1). Repeat, sliding the stitches to the opposite end of the needle, and knit the tube to the desired length.

Three-Needle Bind-Off

With right sides facing, place stitches to be bound off parallel to each other on two needles. Using a third needle, knit one stitch from each needle (two stitches) together (Fig 2.2). Knit the next two stitches together, taking one stitch from each needle. Pass the first stitch over the second stitch. Continue to knit two stitches together and bind off one stitch until the end of the row.

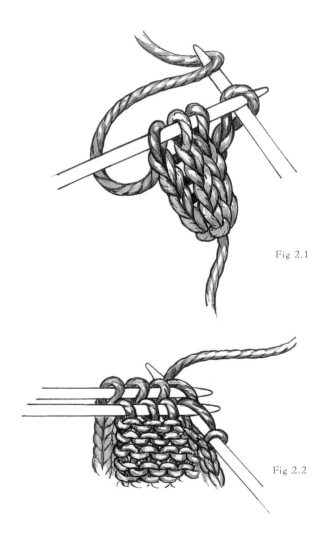

Fig 2.1

Fig 2.2

Fringe

To make fringe, cut a piece of cardboard that is about 3"
(7.6 cm) wide and about 1" (2.5 cm) longer than the desired
length of the fringe. Wind the yarn loosely around the
length of the cardboard until the card is filled or you have
the desired number of fringe pieces. Cut the yarn across the
bottom of the cardboard to produce the fringe. Fold the
strands in half and use a crochet hook to pull the loop end
through the knitted piece as directed. Pull the ends of the
fringe through the loop to tighten the knot. Trim if necessary to make sure the ends are even. Repeat for the remaining fringe pieces.

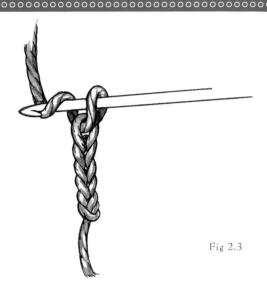

Fig 2.3

Crochet Chain

Make a slipknot and place it on a crochet hook. Wrap the
yarn around the hook and pull the yarn through the loop
(Fig 2.3). Repeat for as many chain stitches as required. To
complete the chain, cut the yarn and pull the end through
the last loop.

Fig 2.4

Single Crochet

Make a crochet chain. Insert the crochet hook into one of
the chains as shown. Draw a loop through the chain using
the hook (two loops on the hook) (Fig 2.4). Wrap the yarn
around the hook again and draw the yarn through both
loops on the hook (Fig 2.5). Repeat for as many stitches
as required.

Fig 2.5

Abbreviations

Here is a list of common knitting and crocheting abbreviations.

beg	begin; beginning; begins		k	knit
bet	between		kfb	knit into the front and then the back loop of same stitch
BO	bind off; binding off; bound off		k2tog	knit two stitches together
CC	contrast color(s)		k3tog	knit three stitches together
ch	chain, as in crochet		kwise	knitwise (as if to knit)
cm	centimeter(s)		m	meter(s)
CO	cast on; casting on		mm	millimeter(s)
cont	continue; continuing; continued		m1	make one stitch (increase). With left needle tip, lift a strand between the needles and form a loop on the left needle. With the right needle, knit into the front of the loop.
dec(s)	decrease(s); decreasing; decreased		oz	ounce(s)
dpn	double-pointed needle(s)		p	purl
foll	follow; following		pfb	purl into front and back of same stitch
fwd	forward		p2tog	purl two stitches together
g	gram(s)		patt(s)	pattern(s)
inc	increase(s); increasing; increased			

pm	place marker
pwise	purlwise (as if to purl)
rem	remain; remaining; remainder
rep	repeat(s); repeating; repeated
rnd(s)	round(s)
RS	right side
sc	single crochet
sk	skip
skp	slip 1 stitch kwise from the left to the right needle. Knit the next stitch. Pass the first stitch over the second stitch (decrease 1 stitch)
sk2p	slip 1, knit two together, pass slip stitch over the knit two together
sl	slip
sm	slip marker
sl st	slip stitch

ssk	slip 2 stitches kwise, one at a time, from the left needle to the right needle. Insert the left needle tip kwise into the back of both slipped stitches and knit them together from this position (decrease 1 stitch)
st(s)	stitch(es)
St st	stockinette stitch
tog	together
WS	wrong side
wyb	with yarn in back of work
wyf	with yarn in front of work
yds	yards
yo	yarn over

Felting Techniques

❀ For the purposes of this book, felting is defined as shrinking a knitted item into a solid piece of fabric, using water, heat, and agitation. This is accomplished with a top-loading washing machine, where floppy knitted items are transformed into sturdy pieces of fiber art. The process is somewhat magical when one considers what the items look like before and after felting. Good felting requires both practice and patience. The techniques shared here are developed from several years of producing hundreds of felted pieces. Over time you will discover what works best for you.

Yarn Selection

A wide range of wool yarns can be used for felting, from scratchy, unprocessed yarns to soft, highly processed ones. Machine-washable wool is not suitable for felting because the yarn has been treated in a way that prevents shrinking, and hence felting. Yarns suggested for patterns in this book range from sport-weight to medium worsted- to bulky-weight wools, all of which should felt well under most conditions. In general, the more processed a yarn, the quicker it will felt. This is because many natural yarns still contain some lanolin, which can slow down the felting process.

One trick is to combine a quick-felting yarn with a slow-felting yarn; the quick-felting yarn will providebase for the slow-felting yarn and speed up the felting process. Also, be careful with using bleached white wool; in most cases it will not felt properly. Try knitting and felting a sample square if you are unsure whether a yarn will felt.

Knitting for Felt

The first task is to find a pattern and start knitting. The patterns in this book are designed for felting, which means they will produce a proportionate shape after shrinking. Knit pieces shrink more, proportionally, in height than in width, so items knit for felting will have an elongated shape. These pieces are also knit on larger needles with a loose knitting gauge to allow room for stitches to soften and form a fabric. In general, the looser the knit, the better the felting. If pieces are knit too tightly, then there is no room for the felt to form, which can produce misproportioned results. If your knitting gauge is much tighter than what is recommended for the patterns in this book, try using a larger needle size to compensate. Also, make a conscious effort to knit in a relaxed fashion, with a loose grip on your needles. Allow the yarn to move freely into your knitted piece. Try a little knitting meditation and you may be surprised how gently the yarn flows.

❀ The test square shown was knitted with one strand of Brown Sheep Nature Spun 100% wool worsted weight in color 108 Cherry Delight and one strand of Brown Sheep Lambs Pride 85% wool / 15% mohair worsted weight in color M102 Orchid Thistle using US size 13 (9 mm) needles. The square was knit with 15 stitches in stockinette stitch for 15 rows.

Measurements: Unfelted Square 8" (20.3 cm) wide × 6" (15.2 cm) high; Final Felted Square: 5" (12.7 cm) wide × 3" (7.6 cm) high

Using Your Washing Machine

Felting can be done in a top-loading washing machine. To conserve water, increase agitation, and speed up the felting process, up to five or six medium-size pieces can be felted at once. Place each item to be felted in a separate laundry bag, the mesh kind used for delicate fabrics. Resist the urge to place knit items to be felted in the washer with normal laundry loads. In most cases, the water temperature used for normal loads is not high enough for the knit pieces to felt properly. The washing machine should be set on the highest water temperature, lowest water level, and highest agitation setting. Begin the wash cycle to fill the washer with water, and add 2–3 tablespoons (30–45 ml) of mild liquid detergent to the water. Set the wash time to the longest setting and stop the washing machine before the drain-and-

1

2

3

Stages in Felting
1: Prefelted square
2: Partially felted square
3: Fully felted square

rinse cycle to check the felting progress. Do not allow the water to drain until each item is completely felted. Wearing rubber gloves, check to see if the stitches have softened and if the pieces have a firm, spongelike texture. If not, then restart the washing machine and run another whole or half agitation cycle, depending upon the progress of each knit piece. Some items will be done prior to others. Take the felted pieces out of the washing machine and place in a bowl until the others are completed. When all have finished felting, place them back into the washing machine and set it to complete a warm rinse-and-spin cycle. Take all of the items out of the washing machine, then shape and remove any stray fibers. Avoid putting felted items in the dryer—the felting process may continue; the pieces will lose their shape and may also develop permanent creases. Let the felted items air dry so they keep their shape. To clean felted items, hand wash with mild detergent, gently squeeze out excess water without wringing, and air dry.

Small items can also be felted by hand using hot water and liquid detergent. Fill a dishpan or sink with hot water and add a little liquid soap. Rub all parts of the knitted item until a firm sponge texture forms. The knitted piece should become dense and it should be difficult to see individual stitches. Rinse the item well with warm water to remove the liquid soap. Squeeze out the excess liquid by wrapping the felted piece in a towel. Shape the item and remove any stray fibers. Allow the item to air dry. Felting by hand takes lots of elbow grease, but can be a very satisfying endeavor if you have the time and tenacity.

Evaluating the Felting

Can pieces be over- and underfelted? The degree to which an item is felted is a personal preference. Some people prefer softer felted items, whereas others prefer more rigid pieces. In general, an item is considered underfelted when it does not hold its shape after drying. However, there are many items, such as scarves or hats, that look wonderful with light felting. Bags or rugs look best when they are felted to the point that they are rigid and hold their shape. But be careful: Items can be overfelted, or shrunk, too much. For example, a tiny purse may look precious, but is not very practical if it can't hold anything. This is especially true for items such as cell phone cases that can shrink to tiny proportions quickly. Make sure to watch these items closely during the felting process. Note that the finished project sizes given for patterns in this book are approximate only and will vary depending upon materials used, felting method, and knitting tension. Remember, felting is not an exact science and many factors can influence the size of the finished piece. Also, every person knits differently and, even if the same materials are used, it is unlikely any two results will look exactly the same. The good news is that every piece produced is one of a kind.

Felted wool bags using hand-dyed yarn:
1: Raspberry Lattice (page 42)
2: Aqua Velveteen (page 40)

Creating Hand-Dyed Yarn

❋ Hand-dyed yarns add a special uniqueness to any knitting project, and this is particularly true for felting. The colors meld during the felting process and combine to produce a hand-painted effect. However, hand-dyed yarns can be very expensive, especially when you need a lot of it for a large felting project. Creating custom hand-dyed yarn is easier than you think, and is less expensive than purchasing it from a yarn shop. All you need are a few kitchen items, dyes, yarn, and a little imagination.

Yarn Selection

Non-washable wool and wool/mohair in a natural color are best for yarn dyeing and can be purchased in bulk at many yarn shops. Follow the same guidelines for purchasing wool for dyeing as you do when purchasing wool for felting, as explained on page 20. Be careful with purchasing bright white wool for dyeing, as bleached wool can be problematic to felt. The unbleached yarns available for dyeing range from a soft white to a light gray. Keep in mind that the base color of the yarn can affect the tone of the dye. Bright, intense colors can be achieved with very light natural shades of yarn, whereas gray bases can produce deep, rich colors. Feel free to experiment with the base color of the yarn used for dyeing to produce a variety of colors and tones.

Dyes for Wool

Acid dyes are typically the first choice for dyeing wool and can be found at many yarn shops and Internet yarn suppliers. These dyes are easy to use and require only vinegar and hot water to set the colors. Their range of colors is extensive, their color combinations only limited by the dyer's imagination. Wool can also be dyed using unsweetened drink mixes, such as Kool-Aid. The colors are bright, and the dyed yarn has a wonderful fruity scent. When picking dye colors, avoid using too many colors per skein of yarn. In this case, less is definitely better. The projects in this book use yarn dyed with a maximum of four colors. Any more, and you run the risk of producing a muddy tone with no distinct color pattern. Color wheels are easy to find at crafts shops and help take the guesswork out of mixing different colors. Try staying in either the cool or warm color family for the majority of the dyes, plus a splash of one dye from another section of the color wheel. For example, use analogous warm colors such as red, orange, and pink, and add violet as the last color.

Wool yarn dyed in cool and warm colors, and undyed yarn

Dyeing with Drink Mixes

An easy way to start yarn dyeing is with unsweetened drink mixes. The process is nontoxic and can be easily accomplished with a few tools from the kitchen. Products such as Kool-Aid contain food-grade dyes, allowing you to use ordinary kitchen utensils and then reuse them for cooking without fear of cross-contamination. However, the process can stain your hands, so make sure to wear plastic or rubber gloves.

There are many ways to mix dyes and apply it to the yarn. Each dyer has her own tips and trade secrets for producing the best color saturation and combinations. The following method has evolved over years of experimenting with Kool-Aid dyeing and has always produced consistent results. Feel free to experiment and develop your own secret methods for dyeing the perfect yarn.

MATERIALS

- 200–250 yds (183–229 m) natural, nonwashable wool or wool/mohair yarn
- 1 package (approximately 0.2 oz [6 g]) each of unsweetened Kool-Aid in four different colors (shown in Cherry, Orange, Pink Lemonade, and Ice Blue Raspberry)
- 12 cups (3 quarts [3 L]) warm water
- 1 cup (250 ml) white distilled vinegar, plus ½ cup (125 ml) if necessary
- 1 large glass bowl
- 4 (8-oz [230 ml]) disposable plastic cups
- Plastic or rubber gloves
- Plastic spoons
- 3-quart (3 L) glass microwave-safe dish
- Microwave oven

Wool yarn dyed with Cherry, Orange, Pink Lemonade, and Ice Blue Raspberry Kool-Aid

1. PREPARING THE YARN

Yarn can be purchased in either balls or hanks. If your yarn comes in a hank, then you are all set for dyeing. If the yarn comes in a ball, then you will need to wind it into a 2' to 3' (61–91 cm) -diameter hank. This can be accomplished using a large rectanglular box. Wind the yarn around the perimeter of the box until you have wound about 200 to 250 yds (183–229 m). Use a figure eight tie to secure each of the yarn ends. Larger or smaller skeins can also be wound, depending upon the needs of the project. Make sure the wool skein fits into the microwave-safe dish and still allows room for the addition of liquids. Add 4 cups (about 1 L) of the warm water and 1 cup (230 ml) of white vinegar to the glass bowl. Place the wool skein in the vinegar solution, fully saturate with the liquid and allow it to soak for at least 15 minutes. Squeeze out the excess liquid and place the wool skein in the microwave-safe dish wrapping the yarn back and forth in an accordion fold.

2. PREPARING THE DYE

Wearing plastic or rubber gloves, prepare one of the Kool-Aid dye solutions by combining one flavor of Kool-Aid and 2 cups (500 ml) of the warm water in one of the plastic cups and mixing well. Repeat, making separate dye solutions in the three other cups, using the three other flavors of Kool-Aid and the remaining warm water. The result is four different-colored dye solutions, each with a volume of 2 cups (500 ml). The total volume of liquid to be added to the yarn skein is 8 cups (about 2 L).

3. APPLYING THE DYE

Each dye solution will be added individually to the yarn in the microwave-safe dish. Pick one dye color and carefully pour the solution onto the wool, taking up only about a quarter of its surface area. Add the dye slowly and try to saturate the area with the color. Pick another dye color and slowly add it to another quarter of the surface area. Repeat the process with the remaining two dye solutions on the remaining areas of undyed yarn. The entire surface of the wool should be covered with the dye. Gently press the dye into the wool with a plastic spoon.

4. SETTING THE COLOR

Place the glass dish in the microwave and heat on high for 15 minutes. Check the liquid to make sure all of the dye has been absorbed. Kool-Aid dye "exhausts" extremely well on wool, meaning all of the dye should adhere to and absorb into the yarn skein, producing a clear liquid in the end. In the rare case that all of the dye does not fix to the wool skein, add an additional ½ cup (125 ml) of white vinegar to the dye bath and microwave for another 15 minutes. Allow the solution to cool, remove the skein from the bowl, and squeeze out the excess liquid by wrapping the yarn in a towel or by placing it in a washing machine set to a gentle spin cycle. Hang the skein and allow it to dry completely. Wind the skein into a ball once it is dry.

Dyeing with Acid Dyes

Wool yarn can also be dyed with acid dyes. The dyes exhaust well and, like unsweetened drink mixes, are fixed on the yarn with vinegar. The process uses kitchen utensils, but the dyes are not food grade. Any utensils used for acid dyeing should not be used again for food preparation or serving. The method for dyeing with acid dyes also differs from that used for drink mixes, in that it involves steaming the yarn in a pot rather than heating it in a microwave oven.

Wool yarn dyed with
Jacquard Acid Dyes in
Violet, Hot Fuchsia,
Turquoise, and Brilliant
Kelly Green

MATERIALS

- 200–250 yds (183–229 m) natural nonwashable wool or wool/mohair yarn
- 1/8 teaspoon each of four acid dyes in four different colors (shown dyed with Jacquard Acid Dyes #614 Violet, #620 Hot Fuchsia, #624 Turquoise, and #627 Brilliant Kelly Green)
- 12 cups (2.8 L) warm water, plus extra for pot
- 1¼ cups (290 ml) white distilled vinegar
- Large glass bowl
- 4 (8-oz [230 ml]) disposable plastic cups
- Plastic or rubber gloves
- 4 plastic spoons
- 8-quart (7.5 L) stainless-steel or enamel pot fitted with a steamer rack 1" (2.5 cm) above the bottom

1. PREPARING THE YARN

Yarn can be purchased in either balls or hanks. If your yarn comes in a hank then you are all set for dyeing. If the yarn comes in a ball, then you will need to wind it into a 2' to 3' (61–91 cm) -diameter hank, as explained on page 29. Combine 4 cups (about 1 L) of the warm water and 1 cup (250 ml) of the white vinegar in the glass bowl. Place the wool skein in the vinegar solution, fully saturate with the liquid, and allow it to soak for at least 15 minutes. Add water to the pot up to the base of the steamer rack (about 1" [2.5 cm] of water and ¼ cup [60 ml] of white vinegar. Remove the wool skein from the vinegar solution and squeeze out the excess liquid. Place the wool skein in the steamer section of the pot, wrapping the yarn in a spiral.

2. PREPARING THE DYE

Wearing plastic or rubber gloves combine 1/8 teaspoon of one dye color with 2 cups (500 ml) of warm water in a plastic cup, and mix well. Repeat with the remaining cups, dyes, and water. The result is four different-colored dye solutions, each with a volume of 2 cups (500 ml). The total volume of dye liquid to be added to the yarn skein is 8 cups (about 2 L).

3. APPLYING THE DYE

Pick one dye color and carefully pour the solution onto the wool, taking up only about a quarter of its surface area. Add the dye slowly and try to saturate the area with the color. Pick another dye color and slowly add it to another quarter of the surface area. Repeat the process on the remaining areas of undyed yarn, with the remaining two dye solutions. The entire surface of the wool should be covered with the dye. Gently press the dye into the wool with a plastic spoon.

4. SETTING THE COLOR

Turn the heat on low and cover the pot. Allow the yarn to steam for 30 minutes, checking often beneath the steamer to make sure the pot does not run out of liquid. Add additional water if necessary. Also check the dye solution toward the end of the heating process to see if most of the dye has been absorbed into the wool skein. If not, steam the yarn for another 15 minutes. Acid dyes typically exhaust very well, as do drink mixtures. Allow the solution to cool, remove the yarn, and squeeze out the excess liquid by wrapping the skein in an old towel or by placing it in a washing machine set to a gentle spin cycle. Hang the wool skein and allow it to dry completely. Wind the skein into a ball once it is dry.

Fabulous Bags

❋ Felted bags are the perfect knitting project to bring on vacation. The yarn requirements are small and all you need is a pair of large needles and a few other notions. You can enjoy some relaxing knitting time and have lots of bags to felt once you return home. Here are four basic bag styles: square, trapezoid, messenger, and evening. Each style has three variations, so you can make essentially the same pattern each time, yet have a totally different look in your finished pieces. Two different sizes are also included in each of the bag patterns, except for the evening bags, which are all small.

The square bags offer a simple shape with lots of room; their accordion-fold handles allow you the flexibility of carrying the bag as a clutch or on your shoulder. The trapezoid bags are similar to the square bags except they have some simple shaping and a little fringe for pizzazz. The messenger bags are just plain fun. They are roomy and perfect for everyday use. The evening bags use beads and lush yarns. These patterns also work very well with hand-dyed yarns, as the yarn requirements are small for each project. Feel free to experiment with different yarn types and dyeing techniques.

○○○○○○○○○○○○○○○○○○○

Bag 1: Sugared Violet (small)
Bag 2: Aqua Velveteen (medium)
Bag 3: Raspberry Lattice (medium)

3

Sassy Square Bags

❀ These square bags offer lots of room, but still maintain a small profile. The strap is one continuous loop that travels through the accordion-folded sides of the bag. You can hold the bag by doubled strap loops, or the strap can be pulled through to one side to produce a shoulder bag. Patterns for small- and medium-size square bags are given here. The small Sugared Violet plays with yarn texture and is made with a mixture of wool and eyelash yarn. (The eyelash yarn is synthetic and will not felt if used alone. If paired with a quick-felting worsted wool, the combined yarns felt easily and produce a furry texture.) Aqua Velveteen and Raspberry Lattice both use wool yarn hand-dyed with acid dyes (see page 30). Start with a natural, unbleached, nonwashable wool and use the dye colors specified for each bag. If you don't have time to dye your own yarn, then purchase a beautiful hand-dyed wool yarn at your favorite knitting shop. The medium-size Aqua Velveteen has mini-cabled sides to reinforce the shape, and eyelash trim on the top. It is great for everyday use and has just enough fluff to be fun for evening. The medium-size Raspberry Lattice is more challenging to knit and incorporates buttonholes through the body of the bag. A felted crochet cord is woven through the holes to create texture and color contrast. Experiment with different color combinations to produce your own unique bags.

FINISHED SIZES

Bag 1: 6" wide × 5.5" high × 3" deep
(15.2 cm wide × 13.9 cm high × 7.6 cm deep)

Bag 2 and Bag 3: 7.5" wide × 6.5" high × 5" deep
(19 cm wide × 16.5 cm high × 12.7 cm deep)

MATERIALS

Yarn

BAG 1

A medium worsted-weight nonwashable wool yarn: total yardage required for colors A and B: 120 yds (224 m) each

A medium worsted-weight polyester eyelash yarn: total yardage required for color C: 98 yds (90 m)

Shown

Brown Sheep Nature Spun 100% wool, worsted weight, 245 yds (224 m) / 3.5 oz (100 g), #207 Alpine Violet (A), #109 Spring Green (B), 1 ball each

Schachenmayr Nomotta Salsa, 100% Polyester, 98 yds (90 m) / 1.75 oz (50 g), #42 Violet (C), 1 ball

BAG 2

A medium worsted-weight nonwashable wool yarn: total yardage required for color A: 327 yds (300 m); total yardage required for color B: 245 yds (224 m); total yardage required for color C: 123 yds (112 m)

A medium worsted-weight polyester eyelash yarn: total yardage required for color D: 30 yds (27 m)

Shown

Austermann Naturwolle 100% wool, worsted weight, 109 yds (100 m) / 1.75 oz (50 g) , #01 Rich Cream: 3 balls, dyed with a combination of Jacquard Acid Dyes #614 Violet, #620 Hot Fuchsia, #624 Turquoise, and #627 Brilliant Kelly Green (A) (See page 30 for instructions on dyeing wool yarn with acid dyes and multiple colors.) Brown Sheep Nature Spun 100% wool, worsted weight, 245 yds (224 m) / 3.5 oz (100 g), #N103 Deep Sea (B), 1 ball, #109 Spring Green (C), 1 ball

Lion Brand Fun Fur, 100% polyester: 60 yds (55 m) / 1.75 oz (50 g), #194 Lime (D), 1 ball

BAG 3

A medium worsted-weight nonwashable wool yarn: total yardage required for color A: 327 yds (300 m); total yardage required for color B: 245 yds (224 m); total yardage required for color C: 123 yds (112 m)

Shown

Austermann Naturwolle 100% wool, worsted weight, 109 yds (100 m) / 1.75 oz (50 g), # 01 Rich Cream: 3 balls, dyed with a combination of Jacquard Acid Dyes in #605 Pumpkin Orange, #614 Violet, #617 Cherry Red, #620 Hot Fuchsia (A) (See page 30 for instructions on dyeing wool yarn with acid dyes and multiple colors.)

Brown Sheep Nature Spun 100% wool, worsted weight, 245 yds (224 m) / 3.5 oz (100 g), #108 Cherry Delight (B), 1 ball, #207 Alpine Violet (C), 1 ball

Needles

US size 13 (9 mm) circular needle, 24" (61 cm) long

US size 13 (9 mm) double-pointed needles, one set 8" (20.3 cm) long

US size K/10.5 (6.5 mm) crochet hook

Notions

4 stitch markers (3 of one color; 1 of a contrasting color)

1 (size 4) sew-in metal snap

Needle and thread

Tapestry needle

Scissors

Gauge (prefelted)

8 stitches and 10 rows = 4" (10 cm) in St st

ABBREVIATIONS

1×1 cable – Knit the second st on the left needle, then knit the first st. Drop both sts from needle.

YARN KEY

BAG 1

(A) Brown Sheep Nature Spun Wool – Violet

(B) Brown Sheep Nature Spun Wool – Spring Green

(C) Schachenmayr Nomotta Salsa Eyelash – Violet

BAG 2

(A) Austermann Naturwolle – Multicolored hand-dyed

(B) Brown Sheep Nature Spun Wool – Deep Sea

(C) Brown Sheep Nature Spun Wool – Spring Green

(D) Lion Brand Fun Fur Eyelash – Lime

BAG 3

(A) Austermann Naturwolle – Multicolored hand-dyed

(B) Brown Sheep Nature Spun Wool – Cherry Delight

(C) Brown Sheep Nature Spun Wool – Alpine Violet

Bag 1: Sugared Violet (small)

Base

With circular needle, CO 16 sts with 2 strands of yarn A and 1 strand of yarn C held together as one.

Knit 20 rows in garter st (knit every row) ending on a WS row. You now have a rectangular piece for the purse base.

Pick up sts around purse base as follows: K16 sts, place marker (pm), pick up and k10 sts along first short side, pm, pick up and k16 sts along second longer side, pm, pick up and k10 sts along second shorter side, and place contrasting color marker. This marker will indicate the start and end of the rounds (52 sts). Slip all markers on each round.

Join, and knit until 8" (20.3 cm), or about 20 rnds, from the base.

Eyelet Holes for Handle

To make eyelet holes for the handle, k3 sts, * yo, k2tog, knit to 5 sts before the next marker, k2tog, yo, k6 sts; rep from * to 5 sts before the last marker, k2tog, yo, k3 sts, and slip the last marker. You should have eight eyelet holes that are spaced 3 sts from each marker.

Knit 2 rnds.

Purl 2 rnds (25 rnds total).

Bind off all stitches loosely pwise. Cut the yarn, leaving a 3" (7.6 cm) tail. Loosely weave in any loose strands securely.

Picot

With size K hook, and 2 strands of yarn B, join with a sl st to the top of the bag. * Sc in the next st, ch 5, and sl st into the first ch. Skip the next st; repeat from * around the top of the bag, ending with a sl st into the last st. Cut the yarn, leaving a 3" (7.6 cm) tail. Loosely weave in any loose strands securely. Follow directions for all styles for making bag handle and finishing (see page 43).

Bag 2: Aqua Velveteen (medium)

Base

With circular needle, CO 22 sts with yarn A and B held together as one.

Knit 32 rows in garter st (knit every row), ending on a WS row. You now have a rectangular piece for purse base.

Pick up sts around purse base as follows: K22 sts, place marker (pm), pick up and k16 sts along first short side, pm, pick up and k22 sts along second longer side, pm, pick up and k16 sts along second shorter side, and place contrasting color marker. This marker will indicate the start and end of the rounds (76 sts). Slip all markers on each round.

Join.

Rnd 1: Knit 1 rnd.

Rnd 2: *Knit 1×1 cable, k18 sts, knit 1×1 cable twice, k12 sts, knit 1×1 cable; rep from * one more time.

Repeat rnds 1 and 2 eleven more times.

Trim

Cut yarn A and B. Attach yarn C and D. Knit 2 rnds (26 rnds).

Eyelet Holes for Handle

To make eyelet holes for handle, k4 sts, * yo, k2tog, knit to 6 sts before the next marker, k2tog, yo, k8 sts; rep from * to 6 sts before the last marker, k2tog, yo, k4 sts and slip the last marker. You should have eight eyelet holes that are spaced 4 sts from each marker.

Knit 2 rnds.

Purl 2 rnds (31 rnds total).

Bind off all stitches loosely pwise. Cut the yarn, leaving a 3" (7.6 cm) tail. Loosely weave in any loose strands securely. Follow directions for all styles for making bag handle and finishing (see page 43).

1. Prefelted Aqua Velveteen
2. Felted Aqua Velveteen

Bag 3: Raspberry Lattice (medium)

Base

With circular needle, CO 22 sts with yarn A and B held together as one.

Knit 32 rows in garter st (knit every row), ending on a WS row. You now have a rectangular piece for the purse base.

Pick up sts around purse base as follows: K22 sts, place marker (pm), pick up and k16 sts along first short side, pm, pick up and k22 sts along second longer side, pm, pick up and k16 sts along second shorter side, and place contrasting color marker. This marker will indicate the start and end of the rounds (76 sts). Slip all markers on each round.

Join, and knit 1 rnd.

○○○○○○○○○○○○○○○○○○
Bag 3: Raspberry Lattice

Rnd 1: *K2 sts, (BO 2 sts, k1 st) four times, BO 2 sts, k1 st, slip marker (sm), k16 sts, sm; rep from * one more time.

Rnd 2: *(K2 sts, CO 2 sts) five times, k2 sts, sm, k16 sts, sm; rep from * one more time. You should have five buttonholes per longer side.

Rnd 3: Knit.

Repeat rnds 1 through 3 seven more times.

Trim

Cut yarn B, and attach yarn C. K2 rnds (26 rnds total).

Eyelet Holes for Handles

To make eyelet holes for handle, k4 sts, * yo, k2tog, knit to 6 sts before the next marker, k2tog, yo, k8 sts; rep from * to 6 sts before the last marker, k2tog, yo, k4 sts and slip the last marker. You should have eight eyelet holes that are spaced 4 sts from each marker.

Knit 2 rnds.

Purl 2 rnds (31 rnds total).

Bind off all stitches loosely pwise. Cut the yarn, leaving a 3" (7.6 cm) tail. Loosely weave in any loose strands securely.

Crochet Cord

Using size K crochet hook, and yarns A and C held together as one, ch 200. Cut yarn, leaving a 3" (7.6 cm) tail, and draw tail through last st. Make two cords, one for each bag side. Follow directions for all bag styles for making the handle and finishing (at right).

○○○○○○○○○○○○○○○○○○
Threading tube handle
through eyelet holes

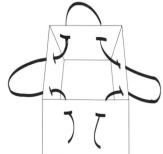

○○○○○○

Square Bag Handles and Assembly
(for all bag styles)

Directions are given first for Bag 1; those for Bag 2 and Bag 3 follow in parentheses.

With size 13 (9 mm) double-pointed needles, CO 3 (4, 4) stitches with 2 strands of wool held together as one (for Bag 1: yarn C, 2 strands; for Bag 2: 1 strand each yarns A and B; for Bag 3: 1 strand each yarns A and C).

K3 (4, 4) sts and move the sts back to the front of the left needle. Wrap the yarn around the back to the front and k3 (4, 4) sts. This will form a small tube, or I-cord (see page 16).

Continue knitting the tube until it is about 40" (45", 45") [101.6 (114.3, 114.3) cm], or desired length. Cut the yarn, leaving a 3" (7.6 cm) tail, and pull through the 3 (4, 4) sts.

Thread the tube handle through the eight eyelet holes on bag body, as shown in the diagram (at left). Start with the right front hole and end with the left front hole. You should have an accordion fold. Before felting, sew the handle ends together loosely, and weave in any loose strands securely (the handle is attached prior to felting to ensure a strong handle and neat eyelet holes).

Felt the bag following the instructions in Felting Techniques, page 22.

For Bag 3 only: Before felting, place the two crochet cords in a separate protective laundry bag to avoid tangling. While the cord is wet, it can be stretched to desired dimensions. Weave the crochet cords through the buttonholes on the front and back of the bag, starting with the top left corner and working to bottom right corner. Tie knots in the cord inside the bag, and cut off and discard any excess cord.

For all bags: Push in the sides of the bag to form an accordion fold, and allow it to air dry. Sew on the metal snap.

6

5

4

Chic Trapezoid Bags

❀ Each of these three fruit-colored felted bags in a trapezoid shape is the perfect accessory to upgrade any outfit to fabulous! Included here are patterns for both small- and medium-size bags. The small Blueberry Belle uses variegated potluck dyed wool in combination with solid wool. Add felted fringe, and you'll have a flirty accessory. The medium-size Strawberry Dream is made from three different colors of sport-weight wool to produce a hand-dyed effect without actually using hand-dyed yarn. The fringe and flower pin give the bag a feminine flair. For the medium-size Blackberry Crush, start saving your scrap balls of wool yarn left over from the other fabulous projects you have made from this book. The balls of yarn are tied together to make one large ball of yarn. The bag is then knit with a combination of the large scrap ball and another wool to produce a unique stripe pattern. Experiment with lots of different colors, and don't worry, the felting process will blend all of the different yarns perfectly.

○○○○○○○○○○○○○○○○○

Bag 4: Blueberry Belle (small)
Bag 5: Strawberry Dream (medium, short)
Bag 6: Blackberry Crush (medium, tall)

FINISHED SIZES

Bag 4: 8" wide (bottom) × 6" wide (top) × 5" high × 3" deep (20.3 cm wide [bottom] × 15.2 cm wide [top] × 12.7 cm high × 7.6 cm deep)

Bag 5: 9.5" wide (bottom) × 8" wide (top) × 5" high × 3.5" deep (24.1 cm wide [bottom] × 20.3 cm wide [top] × 12.7 cm high × 8.9 cm deep)

Bag 6: 9.5" wide (bottom) × 7.5" wide (top) × 6" high × 3.5" deep (24.1 cm wide [bottom] × 19.1 cm wide [top] × 15.2 cm high × 8.9 cm deep)

○○○○○○

Tip: Using Up Scrap Balls of Yarn

Make your own self-striping multicolored wool yarn for felting. Collect small balls of medium worsted-weight wool yarn in different colors. Knot the ends of the yarn together and roll into one large ball. Make sure to use only nonwashable felting wool scraps to make the ball. Any colors can be combined together to produce the stripe pattern.

MATERIALS

Yarn

BAG 4

A bulky-weight nonwashable wool yarn, total yardage required for color A: 201 yds (184 m)

A sport-weight nonwashable wool yarn, total yardage required for color B: 184 yds (168 m)

Shown:

Cherry Tree Hill Potluck 100% wool, bulky weight, 201 yds (184 m) / 4.4 oz (124 g): Jeweltone (A), 1 ball

Brown Sheep Nature Spun 100% wool, sport weight, 184 yds (168 m) / 1.75 oz (50 g), N78 Turquoise Wonder (B), 1 ball

BAG 5

A sport-weight nonwashable wool yarn, total yardage required for colors A, B, and C: 184 yds (168 m) each

Shown:

Brown Sheep Nature Spun 100% wool, sport weight, 184 yds (168 m) / 1.75 oz (50 g), N46 Red Fox (A), N78 Turquoise Wonder (B), 108 Cherry Delight (C), 1 ball each

BAG 6

A medium worsted-weight nonwashable wool yarn: total yardage required for colors A and B: 245 yds (224 m) each

Shown:

Brown Sheep Nature Spun 100% wool, worsted weight, 245 yds (224 m) / 3.5 oz (100 g), N62 Amethyst (A), 1 ball

Scrap balls of 100% wool, worsted-weight yarn knotted together (see tip below), 245 yds (224 m) / 3.5 oz (100 g) (B), 1 ball

Needles

US size 13 (9 mm) circular needle, 24" (61 cm) long

US size 13 (9 mm) double-pointed needles, one set 8" (20.3 cm) long

US size K/10.5 (6.5 mm) crochet hook

Notions

4 stitch markers (3 of one color; 1 of a contrasting color)

1 (size 4) sew-in metal snap

Needle and thread

Tapestry needle

Scissors

For Bag 5: 1 sew-in metal pin backing for flower

Gauge (prefelted)

8 stitches and 10 rows = 4" (10 cm) in St st

YARN KEY

BAG 4

(A) Cherry Tree Hill Bulky – Jeweltone

(B) Brown Sheep Nature Spun Sport – Turquoise Wonder

BAG 5

(A) Brown Sheep Nature Spun Sport – Red Fox

(B) Brown Sheep Nature Spun Sport – Turquoise Wonder

(C) Brown Sheep Nature Spun Sport – Cherry Delight

BAG 6

(A) Brown Sheep Nature Spun Worsted – Amethyst

(B) Worsted-weight wool yarn scraps – Multicolor

Bag 4: Blueberry Belle (small)

Base

With circular needle, CO 24 sts with 1 strand of yarn A and 1 strand of yarn B held together as one.

Knit 20 rows in garter st (knit every row) ending on a WS row. You now have a rectangular piece for the purse base.

Pick up sts around purse base as follows: K24 sts, place marker (pm), pick up and k10 sts along first short side, pm, pick up and k24 sts along second longer side, pm, pick up and k10 sts along second shorter side, and place contrasting color marker. This marker will indicate the start and end of the rounds (68 sts). Slip all markers on each round.

Join, and knit 4 rnds.

Shaping

Decrease rnd: Ssk, knit to 2 sts before next marker, k2tog, sm, k10 sts, sm, ssk, knit to 2 sts before next marker, k2tog, sm, k10 sts, and slip the last marker (64 sts).

Knit 4 rnds and repeat decrease rnd (60 sts).

Knit 4 rnds and repeat decrease rnd (56 sts).

Knit 2 rnds.

Eyelet Holes for Handle

To make eyelet holes for handle, k3 sts, * yo, k2tog, knit to 5 sts before the next marker, k2tog, yo, k6 sts; rep from * to 5 sts before the last marker, k2tog, yo, k3 sts, and slip the last marker. You should have eight eyelet holes that are spaced 3 sts from each marker.

Knit 2 rnds.

Purl 2 rnds (22 rnds total).

Bind off all stitches loosely pwise. Cut the yarn leaving a 3" (7.6 cm) tail. Loosely weave in any loose strands securely.

Fringe and Finishing

From yarns A and B, cut 54 6" (15.2 cm) lengths of yarn from each color.

Starting at any point and using 2 strands for each fringe (1 of each color), attach fringe to the top perimeter of the bag, using crochet hook. Continue attaching fringe around the top perimeter of the bag (10 fringes each per side and 17 fringes each per front and back). (See page 17.)

Follow directions for all bag styles for making the handle and finishing (see page 51).

Bag 5: Strawberry Dream (medium, short style)

With circular needle, CO 30 sts with 1 strand each of yarns A, B, and C held together as one.

Knit 24 rows in garter st (knit every row) ending on a WS row. You now have a rectangular piece for the purse base.

Pick up sts around purse base as follows: K30 sts, place marker (pm), pick up and k12 sts along first short side, pm, pick up and k30 sts along second longer side, pm, pick up and k12 sts along second shorter side, and place contrasting color marker. This marker will indicate the start and end of the rounds (84 sts). Slip all markers on each round.

Join, and knit 4 rnds.

Shaping

Decrease rnd: Ssk, knit to 2 sts before next marker, k2tog, slip marker (sm), k10 sts, sm, ssk, knit to 2 sts before next marker, k2tog, sm, k10 sts, and slip the last marker (80 sts).

Knit 4 rnds and repeat decrease rnd (76 sts).

Knit 4 rnds and repeat decrease rnd (72 sts).

Knit 2 rnds.

Eyelet Holes for Handle

To make eyelet holes for handle, k4 sts, yo, k2tog, *knit to 6 sts before the next marker, k2tog, yo, k8 sts, yo, k2tog; rep from * to last 6 sts, k2tog, yo, k4 sts, and slip the last marker. You should have eight eyelet holes that are spaced 4 sts from each marker.

Knit 2 rnds.

Purl 2 rnds (22 rnds).

Bind off all stitches loosely pwise. Cut the yarn and loosely weave in any loose strands securely.

Fringe and Finishing

From yarns A, B, and C, cut 70 6" (15.2 cm) lengths of yarn from each color. Directions for cutting and attaching fringe are given on page 17. Starting at any point and using three strands for each fringe (one of each color), attach fringe to the top perimeter of the bag using crochet hook. Continue attaching fringe around the top perimeter of the bag (12 fringes each per side and 23 fringes each per front and back).

Follow directions for all bag styles for making the handle and finishing (see page 51).

With 2 strands of yarn C, make a flower pin as shown on page 81.

Bag 5: Strawberry Dream

Bag 6: Blackberry Crush (medium, tall style)

Base

With circular needle, CO 30 sts with 1 strand of yarn A and 1 strand of yarn B held together as one.

Knit 24 rows in garter st (knit every row) ending on a WS row. You now have a rectangular piece for the purse base.

Pick up sts around purse base as follows: K30 sts, place marker (pm), pick up and k12 sts along first short side, pm, pick up and k30 sts along second longer side, pm, pick up and k12 sts along second shorter side, and place contrasting color marker. This marker will indicate the start and end of the rounds (84 sts). Slip all markers on each round.

Join, and knit 4 rnds.

○○○○○○○○○○○○○○○○○
Bag 6: Blackberry Crush

Shaping

Decrease rnd: Ssk, knit to 2 sts before next marker, k2tog, slip marker (sm), k10 sts, sm, ssk, knit to 2 sts before next marker, k2tog, sm, k10 sts and slip the last marker (80 sts).

Knit 4 rnds and repeat decrease rnd (76 sts).

Knit 4 rnds and repeat decrease rnd (72 sts).

Knit 4 rnds and repeat decrease rnd (68 sts).

Eyelet Holes for Handle

To make eyelet holes for handle, k3 sts, yo, k2tog, *knit to 5 sts before the next marker, k2tog, yo, k6 sts, yo, k2tog; rep from * to last 5 sts, k2tog, yo, k3 sts, and slip the last marker. You should have eight eyelet holes that are spaced 3 sts from each marker.

Knit 2 rnds.

Purl 2 rnds (25 rnds).

Bind off all stitches loosely pwise. Cut the yarn and loosely weave in any loose strands securely.

Fringe and Finishing

From yarns A and B, cut 66 6" (15.2 cm) lengths of yarn.

Directions for cutting and attaching fringe are given on page 17. Starting at any point and using 2 strands for each fringe, attach fringe to the top perimeter of the bag using crochet hook. Continue attaching fringe around the top perimeter of the bag (12 fringes each per side and 21 fringes each per front and back).

Follow directions for all bag styles for making the handle and finishing (see right).

Bag Handles (for all bag styles)

Directions are given first for Bag 4; those for Bag 5 and Bag 6 follow in parentheses.

Handle

With size 13 (9mm) double-pointed needles, CO 3 (4, 4) sts with 1 strand of yarn A and 1 strand of yarn B held together as one. K3 (4, 4) sts and move the sts back to the front of the left needle. Wrap the yarn around the back to the front and k3 (4, 4) sts. This will form a small tube, or I-cord (see page 16).

Continue knitting the tube until it is about 35 (40, 40)" [88.9 (101.6, 101.6) cm], or desired length. Cut the yarn, leaving a 3" (7.6 cm) tail, and pull through the 3 (4, 4) sts.

Thread the I-cord handle through the eight eyelet holes on bag body as shown in the diagram on page 43.

Start with the right front hole and end with the left front hole. You should have an accordion fold. Before felting, sew the handle ends together loosely, and weave in any loose strands securely. (The handle is attached prior to felting to ensure a strong handle and neat eyelet holes.)

Finishing (for all bag styles)

Place each bag in a protective laundry bag, and felt according to directions on page 22.

While each piece is wet, it can be stretched to desired dimensions. Push in the sides of the bag to form an accordion fold, and allow it to air dry. Sew on the metal snap.

For Bag 5 only: Sew the metal pin backing to the back of the flower and attach it to the front of the bag.

9

8

Bag 7: Rare Orchid (medium)
Bag 8: Hot Chocolate (medium)
Bag 9: Tangerine Mum (large)

7

Wanderlust Messenger Bags

❋ Messenger bags are the perfect accessory for everyday use. Here are three patterns that incorporate bobbles and fringe. All of the bags have a wide comfy strap and lots of room to carry all of your essentials. The medium-size Rare Orchid is made with a self-striping wool yarn combined with a solid wool and mohair to produce a unique felted pattern. The bobbles on the flap give texture and dimension to the bag, while the fringe adds a funky flair. The medium-size Hot Chocolate is made from variegated thick and thin wool that adds an interesting texture after felting. A companion cell phone case completes the look (see page 57). The large Tangerine Mum is made from wool yarn dyed with Kool-Aid. (Complete instructions on dyeing wool yarn with drink mixes are provided on page 28.) Add a felted flower pin, and you are ready for the day.

FINISHED SIZES

Bags 7 and 8: 9" wide × 7" high × 3" deep
(22.8 cm wide × 17.8 cm high × 7.6 cm deep)

Bag 9: 12" wide × 10" high × 3" deep
(30.5 cm wide × 25.4 cm high × 7.6 cm deep)

MATERIALS

Yarn

BAG 7

A medium worsted-weight wool yarn: total yardage required for color A: 327 yds (299 m)

A medium worsted-weight wool and mohair yarn: total yardage required for color B: 380 yds (347 m)

Shown

Noro Kureyon 100% wool, worsted weight, 109 yds (100 m) / 1.75 oz (50 g), 165A Multicolor (A), 3 balls

Brown Sheep Lambs Pride 85% wool / 15% mohair, worsted weight, 190 yds (173 m) / 4 oz (113 g), M105 RPM Pink (B), 2 balls

BAG 8

A medium worsted-weight wool yarn: total yardage required for color A: 274 yds (251 m); total yardage required for color B: 446 yds (408 m)

Shown

Colinette Hand-Dyed Mezzotint 100% wool, worsted weight, 137 yds (125 m) / 3.5 oz (100 g),76 Lichen (A), 2 balls.
Patons Classic Wool worsted weight, 223 yds (205 m) / 3.50 oz (100 g), 00231 Chestnut Brown (B), 2 balls.

BAG 9

A medium worsted-weight wool yarn: total yardage required for color A: 490 yds (448 m)

A medium worsted-weight wool and mohair yarn: total yardage required for color B: 380 yds (347 m); total yardage required for color C: 190 yds (174 m)

Shown

Brown Sheep Nature Spun 100% wool, worsted weight, 245 yds (225 m) / 3.5 oz (100 g), 730 Natural: 2 balls dyed with a combination of Kool-Aid flavors in Artic Green Apple Blast, Cherry, Orange, and Pink Lemonade (A) (See page 28 for instructions on dyeing wool yarn with Kool-Aid).

Brown Sheep Lamb's Pride 85% wool / 15% mohair, worsted weight, 190 yds (174 m) / 4 oz (100 g), M108 Cherry Delight (C): 1 ball, M188 Tigerlily (B), 2 balls

Needles

US size 13 (9 mm) circular needle, 24" (61 cm) long

US size 13 (9 mm) double-pointed needles, one set 8" (20 cm) long

US size K/10.5 (6.5 mm) crochet hook

Notions

4 stitch markers (3 of one color; 1 of a contrasting color)

1 (size 4) sew-in metal snap

Needle and thread

Tapestry needle

Scissors

Gauge (prefelted)

8 stitches and 10 rows = 4" (10 cm) in St st

Abbreviations

SB (small bobble): (Knit, purl, knit) in next stitch. Turn work. P3 sts. Turn work. Knit all three stitches together.

LB (large bobble): (Knit, purl, knit) in next stitch. Turn work. P3 sts. Turn work. K3 sts. Turn work. P3 sts. Turn work. Knit all three stitches together.

YARN KEY

BAG 7

(A) Noro Kureyon Worsted – Multicolor

(B) Brown Sheep Lamb's Pride Worsted – RPM Pink

BAG 8

(A) Colinette Mezzotint Worsted – Lichen

(B) Patons Classic Wool Worsted – Chestnut Brown

BAG 9

(A) Brown Sheep Nature Spun Worsted – Dyed
   with Kool-Aid

(B) Brown Sheep Lamb's Pride Worsted – Tiger Lily

(C) Brown Sheep Lamb's Pride Worsted – Cherry Delight

Bag Body and Handle (all messenger styles)

Directions are given first for Bag 7; those for Bag 8 and Bag 9 follow in parentheses.

Base

With circular needle, CO 24 (24, 34) sts with 1 strand of yarn A and 1 strand of yarn B held together as one.

Knit 24 rows in garter st (knit every row) ending on a WS row. You now have a rectangular piece for the purse base.

Pick up sts around purse base as follows: K24 (24, 34) sts, place marker (pm), pick up and k12 sts along first short side, pm, pick up and k24 (24, 34) sts along second longer side, pm, pick up and k12 sts along second shorter side, and place contrasting color marker. This marker will indicate the start and end of the rnds (72 [72, 92] sts). Slip all markers on each round.

Join, and knit 9 (9, 14) rnds.

Decrease rnd: K24 (24, 34) sts, slip marker (sm), k2tog, knit to 2 sts before next marker, k2tog, sm, k24 (24, 34) sts, sm, k2tog, knit to 2 sts before next marker, k2tog, and slip last marker (68 [68, 88] sts total).

Knit 9 (9, 14) rnds and repeat decrease rnd (64 [64, 84] sts).

Knit 9 (9, 14) rnds and repeat decrease rnd (60 [60, 80] sts).

Purl 4 rnds. (34 [34, 49]) sts.

Bind off 24 (24, 34) sts removing the first and second stitch markers (36 [36, 46] sts).

Transfer remaining st to a dpn and knit the next 5 sts on the circular needle onto the dpn, for a total of 6 sts. These 6 sts will be used to make the bag strap. Leave the remaining sts on the circular needle.

Bag Strap

Knit 100 rows in garter st, or desired length, on the 6 sts only, using two double-pointed needles ending on a WS row. Transfer the last 6 sts on the circular needle to a dpn. Making sure the strap is not twisted and the dpns are parallel to each other, attach the strap to the other side of the bag. Complete a three-needle bind-off, as shown on page 16, for the 6 sts on both dpns. Remove any remaining stitch markers.

One st remains on the dpn from the three-needle bind-off. Purl across the remaining 24 (24, 34) sts—25 (25, 35 sts) total—for the bag's front flap.

Bag 7: Rare Orchid (medium) Front Flap and Finishing

Flap

Complete the body and strap of Bag 7.

Knit 25 across the flap stitches.

Row 1: K2 sts, p 21 sts, k2 sts.

Row 2: K2 sts, * SB, k3 sts; repeat from * 4 more times, SB, k2 sts.

Row 3: K2 sts, p21 sts, k2 sts.

Row 4: Knit.

Row 5: K2 sts, p21 sts, k2 sts.

Row 6: K4 sts, * SB, k3 sts; repeat from * 3 more times, SB, k4 sts.

Row 7: K2 sts, p21 sts, k2 sts.

Row 8: Knit.

Rep the last 8 rows two more times.

K2 sts, p21 sts, k2 sts.

Knit 4 rows (30 rows total).

Bind off all stitches.

Weave in any loose strands securely.

Fringe

From yarn B cut 86 6" (15.2 cm) strands of yarn. Directions for cutting and attaching fringe are given on page 17. Using two strands for each fringe, attach 15 fringes evenly along the front flap and 14 fringes each along the side flaps.

Finishing

Felt the bag following the instructions on page 22.

While the piece is wet, it can be stretched to desired dimensions. Allow the bag to air dry, and sew the metal snap on the front and front flap.

○○○○○○○○○○○○○○○○○

Bag 7: Orchid Bag

Bag 8: Hot Chocolate (medium) Front Flap and Finishing

Flap

Complete the body and strap of Bag 8.

K12 sts, m1, k13 sts (26 sts).

K2 sts, p22 sts, k2 sts.

Row 1: Knit.

Row 2: K2 sts, p22 sts, k2 sts.

Repeat the last 2 rows eight more times.

K2 sts, * LB, k2 sts; repeat from * six more times. LB, k2 sts.

K2 sts, p22 sts, k2 sts.

Knit 4 rows (28 rows).

Bind off all sts kwise. Loosely weave in any loose strands securely.

Mini Bag

With yarn A and B, make the mini bag following the instructions on page 77.

Finishing

Felt the bags following the instructions on page 22.

While each piece is wet, it can be stretched to desired dimensions. Allow the bags to air dry, and sew the metal snaps onto the bags' fronts and front flaps, and the side and strap of the mini bag.

○○○○○○○○○○○○○○○○

Bag 8: Hot Chocolate with companion mini bag (see page 77 for mini bag pattern)

Bag 9: Tangerine Mum (large)

Flap

Complete body and strap of Bag 9.

Cut yarn B only and attach yarn C.

Knit 35 sts.

K2 sts, p31 sts, k2 sts.

Row 1: Knit.

Row 2: K2 sts, p31 sts, k2sts.

Row 3: K1 st, LB, k31 sts, LB, k1 st.

Row 4: K2 sts, p31 sts, k2 sts.

Row 5: Knit.

Row 6: K2 sts, p31 sts, k2 sts.

Row 7: Knit.

Row 8: K2 sts, p31 sts, k2 sts.

Repeat last 8 rows three more times.

K1 st, * LB, k3 sts, rep from * seven more times, LB, k1 st.

K2 sts, p31 sts, k2 sts.

Knit 4 rows.

Bind off all stitches. Weave in any loose strands securely.

Flower Pin

With yarn A and C make one flower pin, following the Purple and Cherry Carnation instructions on page 80.

Felt the bag and flower pin following the instructions on page 22. While each piece is wet, it can be stretched to desired dimensions. Allow the bag to air dry, and sew the metal snap onto the front and front flap. Attach the flower pin to the front flap.

Bag 9: Tangerine Mum

11

12

10

○ ○ ○ ○ ○ ○ ○ ○ ○ ○ ○ ○ ○ ○ ○ ○ ○ ○

Bag 10: Ruby Sling
Bag 11: Midnight Rendezvous
Bag 12: Silver Fizz

Elegant Evening Bags

✿ Lush yarns, beads, ribbons, and a little sparkle combine to make three fabulous felted evening bags. The Ruby Sling is knit with a hand-dyed bouclé wool yarn and rows of metallic glass beads. The Midnight Rendezvous has a trapezoid shape and is made out of wool and mohair along with a little eyelash yarn at the top. The Silver Fizz is a sparkly clutch with a small strap that can be worn around your wrist; black grosgrain ribbon is woven through the buttonholes to produce an elegant closure at the front flap. These flirty bags will add a little glitz to any fabulous evening out on the town.

FINISHED SIZES

Bag 10: 7.5" wide × 5.5" high (19 cm wide × 13.9 cm high)
Bag 11: 7.5" wide × 5.5" high (19 cm wide × 13.9 cm high)
Bag 12: 8" wide × 5" high (20.3 cm wide × 12.7 cm high)

MATERIALS

Yarn

BAG 10

A medium worsted-weight bouclé wool yarn: total yardage required for color A: 73 yds (67 m)

A medium worsted-weight wool yarn: total yardage required for color B: 73 yds (67 m)

Shown

Berroco Medley 75% wool / 15% acrylic / 10% nylon worsted-weight bouclé, 73 yds (67 m) / 1.75 oz (50 g), 8902 Moulin Rouge (A), 1 ball

Brown Sheep Nature Spun 100% wool, worsted weight, 245 yds (225 m)/ 3.5 oz (100 g), 108 Cherry Delight (B), 1 ball

BAG 11

A medium worsted-weight wool/mohair yarn: total yardage required for color A: 125 yds (114 m)

A medium worsted-weight polyester eyelash yarn: total yardage required for color B: 30 yds (27 m)

Shown

Brown Sheep Lambs Pride 85% wool / 15% mohair, bulky weight, 125 yds (114 m) / 4 oz (113 g), M06 Charcoal (A), 1 ball

Lion Brand Fun Fur 100% polyester, 60 yds (54 m) / 1.75 oz (50 g), 153 Black (B), 1 ball

BAG 12

A medium worsted-weight wool yarn: total yardage required for color A: 120 yds (110 m)

A medium worsted-weight polyester eyelash yarn: total yardage required for color B: 120 yds (109 m)

Shown

Patons Classic Wool, worsted weight, 223 yds (205 m) / 3.50 oz (100 g), 00224 Grey Mix (A), 1 ball

Crystal Palace Fizz Stardust 14% soft metallic fiber, 120 yds (110 m) / 1.75 oz (50 g), 0204 White Ice (B), 1 ball

Needles

US size 13 (9 mm) and 10.5 (6.5 mm) circular needles, each 16" (41 cm) long

US size 13 (9 mm) and 10.5 (6.5 mm) double-pointed needles, one set each 8" (20.3 cm) long

US size K/10.5 (6.5 mm) crochet hook

Notions

Stitch markers

1 (size 4) sew-in metal snap

Needle and thread

Tapestry needle

Scissors

For Bag 10 only: 84 (6 mm) red barrel glass beads

For bag 12 only: 1 yd (91 cm) of $7/8$" (2.1 cm) black grosgrain ribbon

Gauge

Bag 10: 14 stitches and 14 rows = 4" (10 cm) in St st on US size 10.5 (6.5 mm) needle

Bags 11 and 12: 8 stitches and 10 rows = 4" (10 cm) in St st on US size 13 (9 mm) needle

Note: All three of the bags are knit from the top down.

YARN KEY

BAG 10

(A) Berroco Medley Worsted – Moulin Rouge

(B) Brown Sheep Nature Spun Worsted – Cherry Delight

BAG 11

(A) Brown Sheep Lambs Pride Bulky – Charcoal

(B) Lion Brand Fun Fur Worsted – Black

BAG 12

(A) Crystal Palace Fizz Stardust Worsted – White Ice

(B) Patons Classic Wool Worsted – Grey Mix

Bag 10: Ruby Sling

CO 60 sts with yarn A and size 10.5 (6.5 mm) circular needle.

Join, being careful not to twist sts. Place marker for beginning of rnd. Slip marker on all rnds.

Rnd 1: Knit 1 rnd.

Rnd 2: Purl 1 rnd.

Repeat last 2 rnds one more time.

Knit 1 rnd.

String the 84 glass beads onto yarn B. Attach yarn B and knit 1 rnd, making sure to move the beads down the yarn as you knit.

Switch back to yarn A and knit 1 rnd.

Knit 8 more rnds, alternating yarns A and B, and making sure to move the beads along yarn B.

Bead Round

* With yarn B, k4 sts, draw up 1 bead close to the needle and slip the next st pwise with the bead in front of the slipped st; repeat from * eleven more times to the end of rnd.

Knit 9 rnds, alternating between yarns A and B.

Repeat bead rnd with yarn B, pulling up 12 beads total for the rnd.

Knit 9 rnds, alternating between yarns A and B.

Repeat bead rnd with yarn B, pulling up 12 beads total for the rnd.

Knit 3 rnds, alternating between yarns A and B.

Repeat bead rnd with yarn B, pulling up 12 beads total for the rnd.

Repeat the last 2 rows three more times.

Knit 3 rnds, alternating between yarns A and B.

Purl 1 row with yarn B.

Knit 1 row with yarn A.

Using size 10.5 (6.5 mm) double-pointed needles and yarn B, complete a three-needle bind-off of all the sts as shown on page 16.

Bag Strap

Turn the bag right side up. With size K crochet hook and 1 strand of yarn A and 1 strand of yarn B held together as one, sl st to one side of the bag top. Ch st for 50" (127 cm), or desired length. Sl st chain to the other side of the bag, and pull yarn through. Weave in all loose strands securely.

Finishing

Place the bag in a protective washing bag and felt, following the instructions on page 22.

While the piece is wet, it can be stretched to desired dimensions. Allow the bag to air dry, and sew on the metal snap.

Bag 10: Ruby Sling

Bag 11: Midnight Rendezvous

With size 13 (9 mm) circular needle and 1 strand of yarn A and 1 strand of yarn B held together as one, CO 40 sts. Join, being careful not to twist sts.

Place a marker for beginning of rnd, k20 sts, place a contrasting color marker to indicate the middle of the rnd, k20 sts. Slip markers (sm) on all rnds.

Purl 1 rnd.

Knit 1 rnd.

Purl 1 rnd. Cut yarn B and continue knitting with yarn A only.

Knit 4 rnds.

Kfb, knit to 1 st before the next marker, kfb, sm, kfb, knit to 1 st before the next marker, kfb, slip last marker.

Repeat last 2 rnds four more times.

Purl 1 rnd.

Knit 1 rnd.

Using a size 10.5 (6.5 mm) double-pointed needle, complete a three-needle bind-off of all the sts as shown on page 16.

Bag Strap

Turn the bag right side up. With size K crochet hook and yarn A, sl st to one side of the bag top. Ch st for 50" (127 cm) long, or desired length. Sl st to the other side of the bag and pull yarn through. Weave in all loose strands securely.

Finishing

Place the bag in a protective washing bag and felt the bag following the instructions on page 22. While the piece is wet, it can be stretched to desired dimensions. Allow bag to air dry and sew on the metal snap.

○○○○○○

Evening Bag Handle Variations

A wide array of handle styles can be used for the evening bags, so experiment. Try mixing up the handle types. Any of the bags would look sweet with a little loop handle like the Silver Fizz's. You could also make a longer tube and attach it to both sides of the bag so it could sling over your shoulder. All of the bags could be made with no handles and used as clutches. Try adding a long handle to the silver bag—it could be tucked inside the bag and still used as a clutch.

A wide array of purchased handles could also be used, including beaded straps of all lengths. A heavy-weight silver or gold rope purchased at craft store, along with some fancy tassels, would also work well as a handle option for any of the bags. Dress up your little evening bag and be ready for a night on the town!

○○○○○○○○○○○○○○○○○
Bag 11: Midnight Rendezvous

Bag 12: Silver Fizz

Bag Flap

With size 13 (9.5 mm) circular needle and 1 strand of yarn A and 1 strand of yarn B held together as one, CO 20 sts. Knit 1 row and do not join. Turn work.

K2 sts, m1, k16 sts, m1, k2 sts (22 sts).

K2 sts, p18 sts, k2 sts.

K2 sts, m1, k18 sts, m1, k2 sts (24 sts).

K2 sts, p20 sts, k2 sts.

First Buttonhole

K2 sts, m1, k8 sts, BO 4 sts, k7 sts, m1, k2 sts (26 sts total).

K2 sts, p9 sts, CO 4 sts, p9 sts, k2 sts.

K2 sts, m1, k22 sts, m1, k2 sts (28 sts).

K2 sts, p24 sts, k2 sts.

K2 sts, m1, k24 sts, m1, k2 sts (30 sts).

Knit 1 row.

K2 sts, p26 sts, k2 sts.

Second Buttonhole

K13 sts, BO 4 sts, k12 sts.

K2 sts, p11 sts, CO 4 sts, p11 sts, k2 sts.

Row 1: Knit 1 row.

Row 2: K2 sts, p26 sts, k2 sts.

Rep last 2 rows one time more.

Bag Body

K30 sts, CO 30 sts. Join in the rnd. Place a marker for the beginning of the rnd.

Knit 1 rnd.

Purl 1 rnd.

Knit 10 rnds.

Buttonhole row: K13 sts, BO 4 sts, k25 sts, BO 4 sts, k12 sts.

K13 sts, CO 4 sts, k26 sts, CO 4 sts, k13 sts.

Knit 10 rnds.

Third Buttonhole

K13 sts, BO 4 sts, k25 sts, BO 4 sts, k12 sts.

K13 sts, CO 4 sts, k26 sts, CO 4 sts, k13 sts.

Knit 6 rnds.

Purl 1 rnd.

Knit 1 rnd.

Using a size 10.5 (6.5 mm) double-pointed needle, complete a three-needle bind-off of all the sts, as shown on page 16.

Bag Strap

Turn the bag right side up. With size 13 (9 mm) double-pointed needle and 1 strand of yarn A and 1 strand of yarn B held together as one, pick up and k4 sts on the left side of the bag. Knit 4 sts and move the sts back to the front of the left needle. Wrap the yarn around the back to the front and k4 sts. This will form a small tube as shown on page 16. Continue knitting the I-cord until it is about 30" (76.2 cm), or desired length.

Sew the end of the strap back to the left side of the bag to form a circle. Sew in any loose strands.

Place the bag in a protective washing bag and felt according to directions on page 22.

While the piece is wet, it can be stretched to desired dimensions. Allow the bag to air dry.

Pull the ribbon through the buttonholes of the bag, starting with the first hole on the front flap. Continue to weave the ribbon through the buttonholes until you reach the front of the bag. Pull the ribbon over the opening and through the last two buttonholes again. Tie in a bow on the front.

Flirty Accessories

❀ Your fabulous felted bags wouldn't be complete without flirty accessories. Following are patterns for mini bags, flowers, and belts. These are the perfect small projects to bring along on a trip in case the knitting bug strikes. The felted flowers are a cinch to make and are a perfect project for all of those small balls of leftover yarn. They look wonderful on felted bags or attached to your coat or hat. Make a few in bright colors to cheer up those dreary winter days. The mini bags are extremely versatile and will fit cell phones, MP3 players, and any other small items that float around in your purse. There is even one bag that is perfect for your eye- or sunglasses. The geometric belts are formed by a series of squares, circles, and triangles. Three sizes are provided, but try adding or subtracting segments to produce a customized fit. All these accessory projects can be made with small quantities of yarn, so feel free to indulge yourself and use beautiful specialty wool yarns.

○○○○○○○○○○○○○○○○○

Mini Bag 1: Peacock Tote
Mini Bag 2: Hot Pink Baguette
Mini Bag 3: Citrus Slice

Mini Bags

❁ Mini felted bags are fun to make and have lots of uses. Here are three bags that are perfect for organizing all of your small items. The Peacock Tote works great as a cell phone case, and can be used with a larger bag or carried on its own. Its accordion-fold handle can be pulled to one side, and the bag carried around your wrist. The Hot Pink Baguette works great as a stylish eyeglass case and also has an accordion-fold handle. The Citrus Twist has a secure front flap and is perfect for a cell phone or other handheld electronic devices. It can be attached to a larger bag or belt loop, using the side snap. All three can be made to coordinate with the previous felted bags.

FINISHED SIZES

Mini Bag 1: 3.5" wide × 3.5" high × 2.5" deep
(8.9 cm wide × 8.9 cm high × 6.3 cm deep)

Mini Bag 2: 6.5" wide × 3" high × 2.5" deep
(16.5 cm wide × 7.6 cm high × 6.3 cm deep)

Mini Bag 3: 3.5" wide × 3.5" high × 2" deep
(8.9 cm wide × 8.8 cm high × 5 cm deep)

MATERIALS

Yarn

MINI BAG 1

A medium worsted-weight wool yarn: total yardage required for color A and color B: 109 yds (100 m) each

A medium worsted-weight polyester eyelash yarn: total yardage required for color C: 30 yds (27 m)

Shown
Elann Peruvian Collection Highland 100% wool, worsted weight, 109 yds (100 m) / 1.75 oz (50 g), 1520 Precious Turquoise (A), 3681 Carmine Pink (B), 1 ball each

Lion Brand Fun Fur 100% polyester eyelash, 60 yds (55 m) / 1.75 oz (50 g), 112 Raspberry (C), 1 ball

MINI BAG 2

A medium worsted-weight wool yarn: total yardage required for color A and color B: 109 yds (100 m) each

A medium worsted-weight polyester eyelash yarn: total yardage required for color C: 30 yds (27 m)

Shown
Elann Peruvian Collection Highland 100% wool, worsted weight, 109 yds (100 m) / 1.75 oz (50 g), 3681 Carmine Pink (A), 1750 Alpine Violet (B), 1 ball each.

Lion Brand Fun Fur 100% polyester eyelash, 60 yds (55 m) / 1.75 oz (50 g), 191 Violet (C), 1 ball

MINI BAG 3

A medium worsted-weight wool yarn: total yardage required for color A and color B: 120 yds (110 m) each

Shown
Brown Sheep Nature Spun 100% wool, worsted weight, 245 yds (225 m) / 3.5 oz (100 g), N54 Orange You Glad (A), 109 Spring Green (B), 1 ball each

Needles

US size 9 (5.5 mm) circular needle, 16" (41 cm) long

US size 10.5 (6.5 mm) circular needle, 16" (41 cm) long

US size 10.5 (6.5 mm) double-pointed needles, one set 8" (20.3 cm) long

Notions

4 stitch markers (3 of one color; 1 of contrasting color)

1 (size 4) sew-in metal snap

Needle and thread

Tapestry needle

Scissors

Gauge

14 stitches and 14 rows = 4" (10 cm) in St st

Abbreviations

LB (large bobble): (Knit, purl, knit) in next stitch. Turn work. P3 sts. Turn work. K3 sts. Turn work. P3 sts. Turn work. Knit all three stitches together.

YARN KEY

MINI BAG 1

(A) Elann Highland Wool Worsted – Precious Turquoise

(B) Elann Highland Wool Worsted – Carmine Pink

(C) Lion Brand Fun Fur Worsted – Raspberry

MINI BAG 2

(A) Elann Highland Wool Worsted – Carmine Pink

(B) Elann Highland Wool Worsted – Alpine Violet

(C) Lion Brand Fun Fur Worsted – Violet

MINI BAG 3

(A) Brown Sheep Nature Spun Worsted – Orange You Glad

(B) Brown Sheep Nature Spun Worsted – Spring Green

Mini Bag 1: Peacock Tote

Base

With size 10.5 (6.5 mm) needles, CO 16 sts with yarn A. Knit 24 rows back and forth in garter st (knit every row).

You now have a rectangular piece for purse base.

Pick up sts around purse base as follows: K16 sts, place marker (pm), pick up and k12 sts along first short side, pm, pick up and k16 sts along second longer side, pm, pick up and k12 sts along second shorter side, and place contrasting color marker. This marker will indicate the start and end of the rnds (56 sts).

Join and knit 20 rnds. Slip markers on all rnds.

Cut yarn A, and attach yarn B and yarn C. Switch to size 9 (5.5 mm) circular needle and knit 2 rnds.

Eyelet Holes for Handle

To make eyelet holes for handle, k3, yo, k2tog, *knit to 5 sts before the next marker, k2tog, yo, k6 sts, yo, k2tog; rep from * until 5 sts before the last marker, k2tog, yo, k3 sts and slip the last marker. You should have eight eyelet holes that are spaced 3 sts from each marker.

Knit 2 rnds.

Purl 2 rnds.

Bind off all stitches loosely pwise. Cut the yarn and loosely weave in any loose strands securely.

Bag Handle

To make the bag handle, use two size 10.5 (6.5 mm) double-pointed needles. CO 3 stitches with yarn A. K3 sts and move the sts back to the front of the left needle. Wrap the yarn around the back to the front and k3 sts. This will form a small tube as shown on page 16. Continue knitting the tube until it is about 20" (50.8 cm) long, or desired length. Cut the yarn and pull through the 3 sts.

Pull the handle through the eight eyelet holes on the bag body as shown on page 43. Sew the handle ends together loosely before felting, and weave in any loose strands securely.

Felt the bag following the instructions on page 22. While the piece is wet, it can be stretched to desired dimensions. Push in the sides of the bag to form an accordion fold, and allow it to air dry. Sew on the metal snap.

Mini Bag 1: Peacock Tote

Mini Bag 2: Hot Pink Baguette

With size 10.5 (6.5 mm) needles, CO 24 sts with yarn A. Knit 24 rows back and forth in garter st. You now have a rectangular piece for the purse base.

Base

Pick up sts around purse base as follows: K24 sts, place marker (pm), pick up and k12 sts along first short side, pm, pick up and k24 sts along second longer side, pm, pick up and k12 sts along second shorter side, and place contrasting color marker. This marker will indicate the start and end of the rows (72 sts).

Join and knit 4 rnds. Slip markers on all rnds.

Decrease rnd: SKP, k to 2 sts before next marker, k2tog, slip marker (sm), k12 sts, sm, SKP, knit to 2 sts before last marker, k2tog, slip the last marker (68 sts).

Knit 4 rnds and repeat decrease rnd (64 sts).

Knit 4 rnds and repeat decrease rnd (60 sts).

Cut yarn A, and attach yarn B and C. Switch to size 9 (5.5 mm) circular needle and knit 2 rnds.

Eyelet Holes for Handle

To make eyelet holes for the handle, k3 sts, yo, k2tog, *knit to 5 sts before the next marker, k2tog, yo, k6 sts, yo, k2tog; rep from * until 5 sts before the last marker, k2tog, yo, k3 sts, and slip the last marker. You should have eight eyelet holes that are spaced 3 sts from each marker.

Knit 2 rnds.

Purl 2 rnds.

Bind off all stitches loosely pwise. Cut the yarn and loosely weave in any loose strands securely.

Bag Handle

To make the bag handle, use two size 10.5 (6.5 mm) double-pointed needles. CO 3 stitches with yarn A. K3 sts and move the sts back to the front of the left needle. Wrap the yarn around the back to the front and k3 sts. This will form a small tube, or I-cord, as shown on page 16. Continue knitting the tube until it is about 30" (76.2 cm) long, or desired length. Cut the yarn and pull through the 3 sts.

Pull the handle through the eight eyelet holes on the bag body as shown on page 43. Sew the handle ends together loosely before felting and weave in any loose strands securely.

Felt the bag, following the instructions on page 22. While the piece is wet, it can be stretched to desired dimensions. Push in the sides of the bag to form an accordion fold, and allow it to air dry. Sew on the metal snap.

Mini Bag 2: Hot Pink Baguette

Mini Bag 3: Citrus Twist

With size 10.5 (6.5 mm) circular needle, CO 16 sts with yarn A. Knit 20 rows back and forth in garter st (knit every row). You now have a rectangular piece for the purse base.

Base

Pick up sts around the purse base as follows: K16 sts, place marker (pm), pick up and k10 sts along first short side, pm, pick up and k16 sts along second longer side, pm, pick up and k10 sts along second shorter side, and place contrasting color marker. This marker will indicate the start and end of the rnds (52 sts).

Join and knit 10 rnds. Slip markers on all rnds.

Decrease rnd: K16 sts, slip marker (sm), k2tog, knit to 2 sts before next marker, k2tog, sm, k16 sts, sm, k2tog, knit to 2 sts before next marker, k2tog, slip the last marker (48 sts).

Knit 10 rnds and repeat decrease rnd one more time (44 sts).

Purl 4 rnds stopping at the third stitch marker on the last rnd. Remove the third marker and BO 6 sts.

Remove the first marker and BO 16 sts.

Transfer the next 6 sts to a size 10.5 (6.5 mm) double-pointed needle. Leave the remaining sts on the circular needle.

Bag Strap

Knit 40 rows back and forth in garter st on the 6 sts, using both double-pointed needles. Bind off the 6 sts.

Bag Front Flap

Attach yarn B.

K8 sts, m1, k8 sts (17 sts).

K2 sts, p13 sts, k2 sts.

Knit.

K2 sts, p13 sts, k2 sts.

Repeat the last 2 rows 8 more times.

K2 sts, *LB, k3 sts; repeat from * two more times, LB, k2 sts.

K2 sts, p13 sts, k2 sts.

Knit 4 rows and bind off all stitches. Weave in any loose strands securely.

Felt the bag, following the instructions on page 22. While the piece is wet, it can be stretched to desired dimensions. Allow the bag to air dry. Sew on the metal snaps on the handle and the side of the bag, and also on the front flap.

Mini Bag 3: Citrus Twist

1

2

3

○ ○ ○ ○ ○ ○ ○ ○ ○ ○ ○ ○ ○ ○ ○ ○ ○

Pin 1: Berry Posy
Pin 2: Purple and Cherry Carnation
Pin 3: Sherbet Daisy

Felted Flower Pins

FINISHED SIZES

Pin 1: 3" (7.6 cm) diameter

Pin 2: 3" (7.6 cm) diameter

Pin 3: 3.5" (8.9 cm) diameter

MATERIALS

Yarn

PIN 1

A medium worsted-weight wool and mohair yarn: total yardage required for colors A and B: 60 yds (55 m) each

Shown

Brown Sheep Lamb's Pride 85% wool / 15% mohair worsted weight, 190 yds (173 m) / 4 oz (113 g), M100 Supreme Purple (A), M102 Orchid Thistle (B), 1 ball each

PIN 2

A medium worsted-weight wool and mohair yarn: total yardage required for colors A and B: 60 yds (55 m) each

A medium worsted-weight polyester eyelash yarn: total yardage required for color C: 60 yds (55 m)

Shown

Brown Sheep Lamb's Pride 85% wool / 15% mohair worsted weight, 190 yds (173 m) / 4 oz (113 g), M102 Orchid Thistle (A), M108 Cherry Delight (B), 1 ball each

Crystal Palace Fizz 14% soft metallic fiber / 86% polyester, 120 yds (131 m) / 1.75 oz (50 g), 7308 Candy Apple (C), 1 ball

PIN 3

A medium worsted-weight wool and mohair yarn: total yardage required for colors A, B, and C: 60 yds (55 m) each

Shown

Brown Sheep Lamb's Pride 85% wool / 15% mohair worsted weight, 190 yds (173 m) / 4 oz (113 g), M102 Orchid Thistle (A), M105 RPM Pink (B), M188 Tigerlily (C), 1 ball each

Needles

US size 10.5 (6.5 mm) straight or circular needles

US size K/10.5 (6.5 mm) crochet hook

Notions

Metal pin backing 1.5" (3.8 cm)

Needle and thread

Tapestry needle

Scissors

Gauge

14 stitches and 14 rows = 4" (10 cm) in St st

ABBREVIATIONS

w&t (wrap and turn): Sl st with yarn in front to right needle, wrap yarn around st to back, turn to wrong side and move st back to right needle with yarn in front.

YARN KEY

PIN 1

(A) Brown Sheep Nature Spun Worsted – Supreme Purple

(B) Brown Sheep Nature Spun Worsted – Orchid Thistle

PIN 2

(A) Brown Sheep Nature Spun Worsted – Orchid Thistle

(B) Brown Sheep Nature Spun Worsted –Cherry Delight

(C) Crystal Palace Fizz Worsted – Candy Apple

PIN 3

(A) Brown Sheep Nature Spun Worsted – Orchid Thistle

(B) Brown Sheep Nature Spun Worsted – RPM Pink

(C) Brown Sheep Nature Spun Worsted – Tigerlily

Pin 1: Berry Posy

With size K crochet hook, ch 5 with 2 strands of yarn A held together as one.

Sl st in the first ch to form a loop. Work 10 sc in ch loop. Sl st in front loop of first sc.

* Ch 5 and sl st in the front loop of the next sc; rep from * nine more times. Turn work over.

Cut yarn A, and attach yarn B.

With yarn B, sl st into the remaining loop of first sc.

** Ch 7 and sl st into the remaining loop of the next sc; repeat from ** nine more times.

*** Ch 9 and sl st around the post of the next sc; rep from *** nine more times.

Pull yarn strands through last sl st, and cut yarn. Weave in any loose strands securely.

Felt the flower, following the instructions on page 22. After felting and air drying, sew on pin backing.

Pin 2: Purple and Cherry Carnation

With size 10.5 (6.5 mm) needle, CO 5 sts with 2 strands of yarn A held together as one. BO 3 sts and k1.

* K2, and CO 3 sts, BO 3 sts and k1; repeat from * eight more times.

Cut yarn A and attach yarn B and yarn C.

** K2 and CO 5 sts, BO 5 sts and k1; repeat from ** thirteen more times.

K2 and CO 5 sts. BO 7 sts. Cut yarn, leaving an 8" (20.3 cm) tail to sew flower together.

Roll the piece into a flower with the eyelash knit on the outside. Secure the roll by sewing loosely through the center with yarn. Weave in any loose strands securely.

Felt the flower, following the instructions on page 22. After felting and air drying, sew on pin backing.

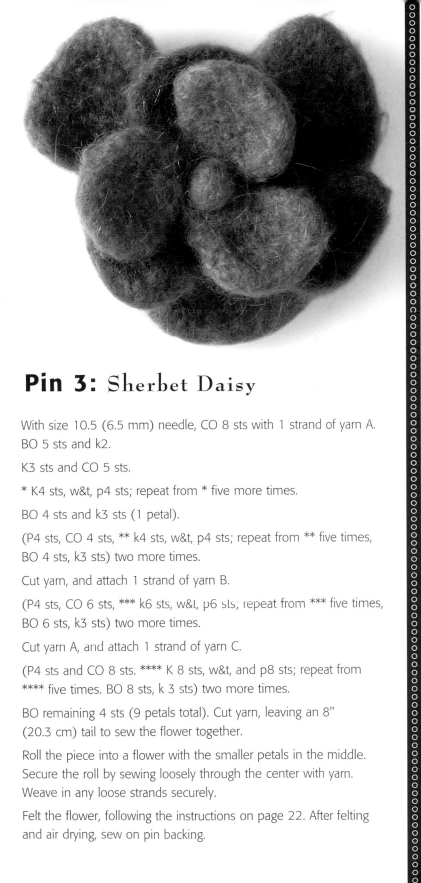

Pin 3: Sherbet Daisy

With size 10.5 (6.5 mm) needle, CO 8 sts with 1 strand of yarn A. BO 5 sts and k2.

K3 sts and CO 5 sts.

* K4 sts, w&t, p4 sts; repeat from * five more times.

BO 4 sts and k3 sts (1 petal).

(P4 sts, CO 4 sts, ** k4 sts, w&t, p4 sts; repeat from ** five times, BO 4 sts, k3 sts) two more times.

Cut yarn, and attach 1 strand of yarn B.

(P4 sts, CO 6 sts, *** k6 sts, w&t, p6 sts; repeat from *** five times, BO 6 sts, k3 sts) two more times.

Cut yarn A, and attach 1 strand of yarn C.

(P4 sts and CO 8 sts. **** K 8 sts, w&t, and p8 sts; repeat from **** five times. BO 8 sts, k 3 sts) two more times.

BO remaining 4 sts (9 petals total). Cut yarn, leaving an 8" (20.3 cm) tail to sew the flower together.

Roll the piece into a flower with the smaller petals in the middle. Secure the roll by sewing loosely through the center with yarn. Weave in any loose strands securely.

Felt the flower, following the instructions on page 22. After felting and air drying, sew on pin backing.

Geometric Belts

❀ Geometric shapes, bright colors, and beads are used to make these felted belts. The Chai Latte uses a soft, hand-painted yarn that felts quickly to produce a nubby texture. It is knit from a series of circles with holes in between, and is fastened with crocheted chains. The Sapphire Moon is made in similar fashion but uses a series of triangles with holes in between. The Sunset Strip showcases a rainbow of colored yarn. Knitting a series of squares with holes in between makes the belt; crochet chains are used to tie it. All of the belts, given here in one size each, can be made shorter or longer by subtracting or adding geometric segments. Make all three to coordinate with a variety of outfits.

FINISHED SIZES

Belt 1: (small) 2.5" wide × 28" long
(6.4 cm wide × 71.1 cm long)

Belt 2: (medium) 2.5" wide × 30" long
(6.4 cm wide × 76.2 cm long)

Belt 3: (large) 2.5" wide × 32" long
(6.4 cm wide × 81.3 cm long)

ooooooooooooooooo

Belt 1: Chai Latte
Belt 2: Sapphire Moon
Belt 3: Sunset Strip

MATERIALS

Yarn

BELT 1

A medium worsted-weight nonwashable wool yarn: total yardage required: 109 yds (100 m)

Shown

Noro Kureyon 100% wool, worsted weight, 109 yds (100 m) / 1.75 oz (50 g), 165A Multicolor, 1 ball

BELT 2

A medium worsted-weight nonwashable wool yarn: total yardage required: 137 yds (125 m)

Shown

Colinette Hand-Dyed Mezzotint 100% wool, worsted weight, 137 yds (125 m) / 3.5 oz (100 g), 76 Lichen, 1 ball

BELT 3

A medium worsted-weight nonwashable wool yarn: total yardage required: 138 yds (126 m)

Shown

Classic Elite Waterspun 100% merino wool, worsted weight, 138 yds (126 m) / 1.75 oz (50 g), 2549 Periwinkle, 1 ball

Needles

US size 10.5 (6.5 mm) straight needles

US size I/9 (5.5 mm) crochet hook

Notions

Tapestry needle

Scissors

For Belt 1 and Belt 3: 12 (6 mm) plastic pony beads

For Belt 2: 4 (8 mm) round glass beads

Gauge

14 stitches and 14 rows = 4" (10 cm) in St st

YARN KEY

BELT 1

(A) Noro Kureyon Worsted – Multicolored

BELT 2

(A) Colinette Mezzotint Worsted – Lichen

BELT 3

(A) Classic Elite Waterspun Worsted – Periwinkle

Belt 1: Chai Latte (small)

Directions for small, medium, and large belt sizes are given. The width for each belt is given in the instructions. Medium and large directions for length are shown in parentheses.

With straight needles, CO 6 sts with 1 strand of yarn A.

Circle Motif

Rows 1–2: Knit 2 rows.

Row 3: K1 st, m1, k4 sts, m1, k1 st (8 sts).

Row 4: Knit 1 row.

Row 5: K1 st, m1, k6 sts, m1, k1 st (10 sts).

Rows 6–10: Knit 5 rows.

Row 11: Knit 2 sts, BO 6 sts, k1 st.

Row 12: Knit 2 sts, CO 6 sts, k2 sts.

Rows 13–16: Knit 4 rows.

Row 17: K1 st, skp, k4 sts, k2tog, k1 st (8 sts).

Row 18: Knit 1 row.

Row 19: K1 st, skp, k2 sts, k2tog, k1 st (6 sts).

Row 20: Knit 1 row.

Repeat the last 20 rows for circle motif, 5 (6, 7) more times, or to desired length.

Bind off all stitches.

Ties

* With crochet hook, ch 75 and sl st to the side of the first circle of the belt. Single crochet along the length of belt to the end. Sl st to the last st and ch 75, cut yarn and pull through the last ch st. Rep from * for second side, attaching that crocheted chain to the last circle of the belt.

Place the belt in a protective laundry bag, and felt following the instructions on page 22. While the piece is wet, it can be stretched to desired dimensions. Place 1 glass bead on the end of each tie, knot, and use as a closure for the belt.

Belt 1: Chai Latte

○○○○○○○○○○○○○○○○○
Belt 3: Sapphire Moon

Belt 2: Sapphire Moon (medium)

Directions for small, medium, and large belt sizes are given. The width for each belt is given in the instructions. Medium and large directions for length are shown in parentheses.

With straight needles, CO 2 sts with 1 strand of yarn A.

Triangle Motif

Row 1: Kfb of both sts (4 sts).

Row 2: Knit 1 row.

Row 3: K1 st, m1, k2 sts, m1, k1 st (6 sts).

Row 4: Knit 1 row.

Row 5: K1 st, m1, k4 sts, m1, k1 st (8 sts).

Row 6: Knit 1 row.

Row 7: K1 st, m1, k6 sts, m1, k1 st (10 sts).

Row 8: Knit 1 row.

Row 9: K1 st, m1, k6 sts, m1, k1 st (12 sts).

Row 10: Knit 1 row.

Row 11: K3 sts, BO 6 sts, k2 sts.

Row 12: K3 sts, CO 6 sts, k3 sts.

Rows 13–14: Knit 2 rows.

Row 15: K1 st, skp, k6 sts, k2tog, k1 st (10 sts).

Row 16: Knit 1 row.

Row 17: K1 st, skp, k4 sts, k2tog, k1 st (8 sts).

Row 18: Knit 1 row.

Row 19: K1 st, skp, k2 sts, k2tog, k1 st (6 sts).

Row 20: Knit 1 row.

Row 21: K1 st, skp, k2tog, k1 st (4 sts).

Row 22: Knit 1 row.

Row 23: K2tog twice (2 sts).

Row 24: Knit 1 row.

Repeat last 24 rows for triangle motif, 5 (6, 7) times, or to desired length.

Bind off all stitches.

Ties

* With crochet hook, ch 75 and sl st to the side of the first triangle of the belt. Single crochet along the length of belt to the end. Sl st to the last st and ch 75, cut yarn and pull through the last ch st. Rep from * for second side, attaching that crocheted chain to the last triangle of the belt.

Place the belt in a protective laundry bag, and felt following the instructions on page 22. While the piece is wet, it can be stretched to desired dimensions. Place 3 plastic pony beads each on the ends of the ties, knot, and use as a closure for the belt.

Belt 3: Sunset Strip (large)

Directions for small, medium, and large belt sizes are given. The width for each belt is given in the instructions. Medium and large directions for length are shown in parentheses.

With straight needles, CO 10 sts with 1 strand of yarn A.

Square Motif

Rows 1–10: Knit 10 rows back and forth in garter st (knit every row).

Row 11: K2 sts, BO 6 sts, k1 st.

Row 12: K2 sts, CO 6 sts, k2 sts.

Repeat the last 12 rows for square motif, 10 (11, 12) more times or to desired length.

Knit 10 rows. Bind off all stitches.

Ties

* With crochet hook, ch 75 and sl st to the top right corner of the belt. Single crochet along the length of belt to the end. Sl st to the last st and ch 75, cut yarn and pull through the last ch st. Rep from * for second side, attaching that crocheted chain to the last square of the belt.

Place the belt in a protective laundry bag, and felt following the instructions on page 22. While the piece is wet, it can be stretched to desired dimensions. Place 3 plastic pony beads on the end of each tie, knot, and use as a closure for the belt.

Belt 3: Sunset Strip

Fun Felted
Home Decor

❀ There is nothing cozier than felted wool for the home. It is soft, durable, and surprisingly easy to care for. It will hold up to the rigors of both children and pets. The felted table setting is perfect for a large party or an intimate dinner at home. The beaded trim adds a lovely contrasting texture. (Sew a matching tablecloth and napkins, and you are all set!) The felted rugs are a comfortable addition to any room and are really fun to make. They are constructed from modular knit and mitered blocks: each new block is added to the last completed one. The projects go quick, as they use large needles and thick yarn. With this method, it is easy to produce a good-size rug for any room in your home. The final project in this book is in honor of our furry friends: Make a special bed or toy for your favorite cat or dog. A pet will love the felted wool, especially if you place it in a sunny spot.

Table Toppers

 Circular shapes and colorful beads are used to make this felted table setting. The circular place mat has a hole in the center and a ruffled and beaded edge. The coaster is also circular and has a beaded edge. A small I-cord and more beads make the napkin ring. The place setting is knit using a bulky wool and mohair yarn that produces a furry texture after felting. The plastic pony beads are easy to string on to the yarn and won't tax your budget. Make as many place settings as you like and enjoy rave reviews from your dinner guests.

FINISHED SIZES

Place Mat: 15" diameter (38.1 cm)

Coaster: 5.5" diameter (13.9 cm)

Napkin Ring: 3" diameter (7.6 cm)

Ruffled Place Mat, Beaded Coaster, and Beaded Napkin Ring

MATERIALS

Yarn

PLACE MAT, COASTER, AND NAPKIN RING

A bulky-weight wool and mohair yarn: yardage required for colors A and B: 125 yds (114 m) each

Shown

Brown Sheep Lamb's Pride 85% wool / 15% mohair, single-ply, bulky weight, 125 yds (114 m) / 4 oz (113 g), M62 Amethyst (A), M65 Sapphire (B), 1 ball each

Needles

US size 13 (9 mm) circular needles, one each 16" (41 cm), and 24" (61 cm) long

US size 13 (9 mm) double-pointed needles, one set 8" (20.3 cm) long

US size K/10.5 (6.5 mm) crochet hook

Notions

Tapestry needle

Scissors

240 (208 for nonruffled version) (6 mm) plastic pony beads per three-piece place setting

Gauge

8 stitches and 10 rows = 4" (10 cm) in St st

YARN KEY

PLACE MAT, COASTER, AND NAPKIN RING

(A) Brown Sheep Lamb's Pride Bulky – Amethyst

(B) Brown Sheep Lamb's Pride Bulky – Sapphire

Ruffled Place Mat
(worked in the round)

With 16" (41 cm) circular needle, and 1 strand of yarn A, CO 32 sts. Join, being careful not to twist stitches.

Knit 1 rnd.

Purl 1 rnd.

Knit 3 rnds.

Increase Rnd 1: Kfb of each st to the end of the rnd (64 sts). Change to 24" (61 cm) circular needle.

Knit 7 rnds. Cut yarn A, and attach yarn B.

Increase Rnd 2: Kfb of each st to the end of the rnd (128 sts). To produce a nonruffled place mat, kfb of every other st (96 sts).

Knit 7 rnds.

Purl 1 rnd.

BO all stitches loosely.

Weave in any loose strands securely.

String 32 pony beads on to yarn B. With wrong side facing, and using crochet hook and yarn B, sc around the inside of the hole in the place mat, placing a bead on each cast-on st.

String 128 pony beads on to yarn B (96 pony beads for nonruffled version). With wrong side facing, using crochet hook and yarn B, sc around the outside of the place mat, placing a bead on each bound-off st.

Finishing

Place the mat in a protective laundry bag, and felt following the directions on page 22.

While the piece is wet, it can be stretched to desired dimensions. Allow the place mat to air dry.

Ruffled Place Mat

Beaded Coaster
(worked in the round)

With double-pointed needles, and 1 strand of yarn B, CO 8 sts. Place marker at beginning of round.

Being careful not to twist sts, join and knit 1 rnd.

Increase Rnd 1: Kfb of each st to the end of the rnd (16 sts).

Knit 3 rnds.

Increase Rnd 2: Kfb of each st to the end of the rnd (32 sts).

Purl 1 rnd.

Knit 4 rnds.

Purl 1 rnd.

Bind off all stitches.

Weave in any loose strands securely.

String 32 pony beads on to yarn B. With wrong side facing, and using crochet hook and yarn B, sc around outside of the coaster, placing a bead on each bound-off st.

Finishing

Place the coaster in a protective laundry bag, and felt according to directions on page 22.

While the piece is wet, it can be stretched to desired dimensions. Allow the coaster to air dry.

Beaded Coaster

Beaded Napkin Ring
(worked using I-cord technique)

String 48 pony beads on to yarn B. Using two double-pointed needles and yarn B, CO 4 sts.

Work I-cord as shown on page 16.

Knit 1 row.

Knit 1 row using 1 pony bead per stitch.

Repeat the last 2 rows eleven more times.

Cut the yarn and pull the end through the 4 sts.

Loosely sew the cast-on and bind-off ends of the I-cord together to make a ring.

Weave in any loose strands securely.

Finishing

Place the napkin ring in a protective laundry bag, and felt according to directions on page 22.

While the piece is wet, it can be stretched to desired dimensions. Allow the napkin ring to air dry.

Beaded Napkin Ring

Planet Earth Rugs

✿ Earthy colors and modular knitting are used to make these felted rugs. Since all of the rugs are knit using garter stitch on big needles, you will be ready for felting in no time. Earth is knit with an eco-friendly wool and hemp–blend yarn that felts beautifully. Water is knit with a combination of bulky and worsted-weight wool. This has the effect of producing a larger rug without increasing the number of knit squares. Fire is a mix of orange, red, and pink, and is the perfect item to brighten any room. Feel free to add on more squares if you would like to produce a larger rug.

FINISHED SIZES

Rug 1: 20" (50.8 cm) wide × 25" (63.5 cm) long

Rug 2: 25" (63.5 cm) wide × 31" (78.7 cm) long

Rug 3: 35" (88.9 cm) wide × 28" (71.1 cm) long

MATERIALS

Yarn

RUG 1

A medium worsted-weight wool yarn: total yardage required for colors A, B, and C: 245 yds (224 m) each

A medium worsted-weight hemp and wool yarn: total yardage required for color D: 750 yds (686 m)

Shown

Brown Sheep Nature Spun 100% wool, worsted weight, 245 yds (224 m) / 3.5 oz (100 g), N03 Grey Heather (A), 601 Pepper (B), 880 Charcoal (C), 1 ball each

Hemp Traders 55% hemp and 45% wool, worsted weight, 250 yds (227 m) / 4 oz (113 g), 01 Natural (D), 3 balls

RUG 2

A bulky-weight wool yarn: total yardage required for colors A and B: 402 yds (368 m) each

A medium worsted-weight wool and mohair yarn: total yardage required for color C: 760 yds (695 m)

Shown

Cherry Tree Hill Potluck 100% wool, bulky weight, 201 yds (184 m) / 4.4 oz (124 g), Blue and Green (A), Jeweltone (B), 2 balls each

Brown Sheep Lamb's Pride 85% wool / 15% mohair, single-ply, worsted weight, 190 yds (174 m) / 4 oz (113 g), 117 Winter Blue (C), 4 balls

RUG 3

A medium worsted-weight wool yarn: total yardage required for colors A, B, and C: 478 yds (437 m) each, total yardage required for color D: 1,110 yds (1,015 m)

Shown

Cascade Ecological 100% wool, worsted weight, 478 yds (437 m) / 8.8 oz (250 g), 2749 Orange (A), 8447 Red (B), 8456 Pink (C), 1 ball each

Plymouth Outback 100% wool, worsted weight, 370 yds (338 m) / 8 oz (227 g), 913 Red Mix (D), 3 balls

Needles

For Rug 1: US size 13 (9 mm) circular needle, 24" (61 cm) long

For Rug 2 and Rug 3: US size 15 (12 mm) circular needle, 24" (61 cm) long

US size K/10.5 (6.5 mm) crochet hook

Notions

Tapestry needle

Scissors

Gauge

8 stitches and 10 rows = 4" (10 cm) in St st

YARN KEY

RUG 1

(A) Brown Sheep Nature Spun Worsted – Grey Heather

(B) Brown Sheep Nature Spun Worsted – Pepper

(C) Brown Sheep Nature Spun Worsted – Charcoal

(D) Hemp Traders Hemp and Wool Worsted – Natural

RUG 2

(A) Cherry Tree Hill Potluck Bulky – Blue and Green

(B) Cherry Tree Hill Potluck Bulky – Jeweltone

(C) Brown Sheep Lamb's Pride Worsted – Winter Blue

RUG 3

(A) Cascade Ecological Wool Worsted – Orange

(B) Cascade Ecological Wool Worsted – Red

(C) Cascade Ecological Wool Worsted – Pink

(D) Plymouth Outback Wool Worsted – Red Mix

Rug Body (for all rugs)

Directions are given for both small and medium-size rugs. All of the mitered squares for the rug are knit in garter st (knit every row).

With circular needle and 2 strands of yarn held together as one, CO 31 sts and knit 1 row.

SQUARE A (CHART 1, PAGE 99)

Row 1: K14 sts, sk2p, k14 sts.

Row 2: Knit 1 row.

Row 3: K13 sts, sk2p, k13 sts.

Row 4: Knit 1 row.

Row 5: K12 sts, sk2p, k12 sts.

Row 6: Knit 1 row.

Row 7: K11 sts, sk2p, k11 sts.

Row 8: Knit 1 row.

Row 9: K10 sts, sk2p, k10 sts.

Row 10: Knit 1 row.

Row 11: K9 sts, sk2p, k9 sts.

Row 12: Knit 1 row.

Row 13: K8 sts, sk2p, k8 sts.

Row 14: Knit 1 row.

Row 15: K7 sts, sk2p, k7 sts.

Row 16: Knit 1 row.

Row 17: K6 sts, sk2p, k6 sts.

Row 18: Knit 1 row.

Row 19: K5 sts, sk2p, k5 sts.

Row 20: Knit 1 row.

Row 21: K4 sts, sk2p, k4 sts.

Row 22: Knit 1 row.

Row 23: K3 sts, sk2p, k3 sts.

Row 24: Knit 1 row.

Row 25: K2 sts, sk2p, k2 sts.

Row 26: Knit 1 row.

Row 27: K1 st, sk2p, k1 st.

Row 28: K3tog. Do not bind off.

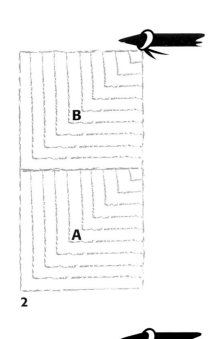

2

1

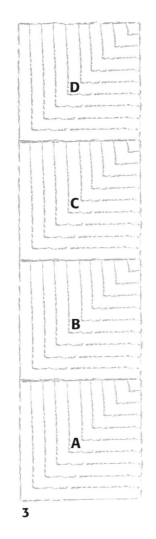

3

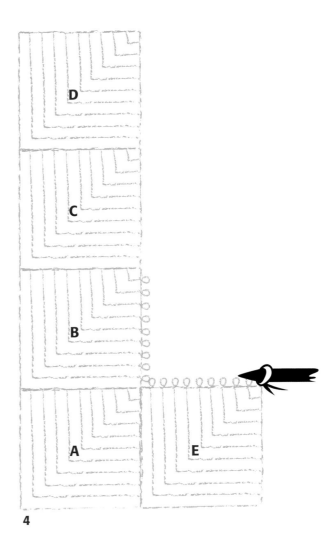

4

SQUARE B (CHART 2)

With RS facing, use stitch on needle as first st, pick up and knit 14 sts along the top of the first knit square (15 sts).

CO 16 sts; turn and knit 1 row. Repeat the 28 rows of Square A.

SQUARE C (CHART 3)

Repeat directions for Square B.

SQUARE D (CHART 4)

Repeat directions for Square B.

FOR SMALL SIZE ONLY

Cut yarn and pull through the last stitch. One panel of squares is now complete.

CO 15 sts.

With RS facing pick up and knit 16 sts along the right side of Square A (for Square E, shown above in chart 4).

Repeat directions for Squares A through D to complete panels 2, 3, 4, and 5. You will have a total of twenty knit squares with five panels of four squares each, as shown on page 100.

FOR MEDIUM SIZE ONLY

Make one more square, repeating directions for Square B.

Cut yarn and pull through the last stitch. One panel of squares is now complete.

CO 15 sts.

With RS facing pick up and knit 16 sts along the right side of Square A.

Repeat directions for Squares A through E to make panels 2, 3, 4, 5, and 6. You will have a total of thirty knit squares with six panels of five squares each, as shown on page 102.

Finishing

With crochet hook and 2 strands of yarn, single crochet around entire perimeter of the rug.

Felt the rug according to directions on page 22.

After felting, the rug can be stretched to the desired dimensions.

Allow the rug to air dry.

Rug 1

Follow directions for the small rug, using the color chart shown and yarns A, B, C, and D. Use size 13 (9 mm) circular needle and 1 strand each of hemp/wool and wool yarn held together as one. Use yarn colors B and D to crochet around the rug.

Rug 2

Follow directions for the small rug, using the color chart shown and yarns A, B, and C. Use size 15 (12 mm) circular needle and 1 strand each of worsted- and bulky-weight wool yarn held together as one. Use yarn colors B and C to crochet around the rug.

Color Chart for Rug 1

 Yarn colors A & D   Yarn colors B & D

Yarn colors C & D

Color Chart for Rug 2

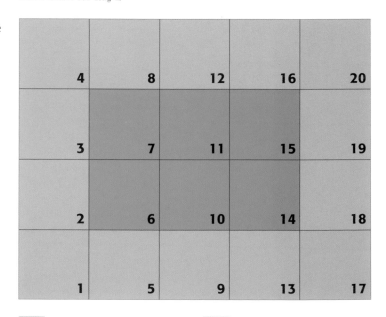

Yarn colors A & C   Yarn colors B & C

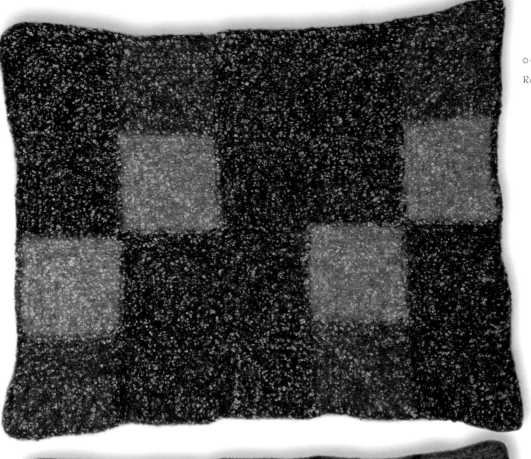

Rug 1: Earth

Rug 2: Water

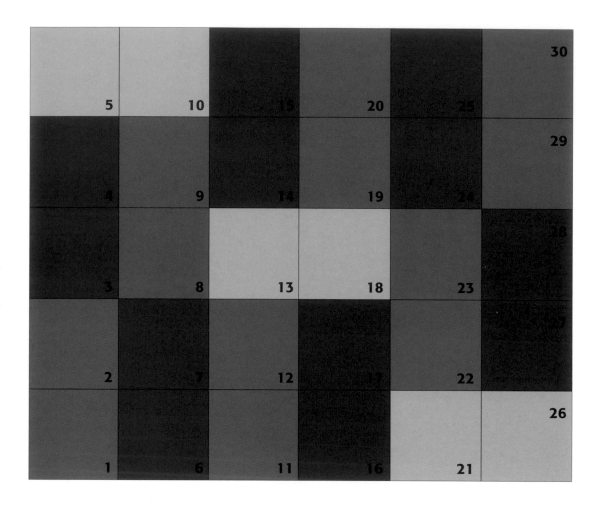

 Yarn colors A & D

Yarn colors B & D

 Yarn colors C & D

Rug 3

Follow directions for the medium-size rug using the color chart shown and yarns A, B, C, and D. Use size 15 (12 mm) circular needle and 1 strand each of worsted-weight wool yarn held together as one. Use yarn colors B and D to crochet around the rug.

○○○○○○○○○○○○○○○○○

Rug 3: Fire

○○○○○○○○○○○○○○○○○

1. Violet's Bed
2. Storm's Cat Toy
3. Simon's Dog Toy

For Furry Friends

❀ What could be more perfect than a felted bed and toy for your favorite furry friend? This set is named in honor of my three cats. Violet's Bed is very easy to make and supercozy. Place the bed in a sunny spot and be ready for loud purring. The pet bed can also accommodate a small dog. Storm's Cat Toy is a felted fish with a handle and bell. It is the perfect project for all of those small balls of scrap wool yarn hanging around. Simon is also a cat, but he likes to play with squeaky toys, so I don't think he will mind being a dog toy's namesake. This dog toy has a handle and two plastic squeakers on either end. Have fun indulging your furry friends by making all three projects.

FINISHED SIZES

Pet Bed: 12" (30.4 cm) wide × 15" (38.1 cm) long × 3.5" high (8.9 cm)

Cat Toy: 3" (7.6 cm) wide × 8" (20.3 cm) long; handle 12" (30.4 cm)

Dog Toy: 3" (7.6 cm) wide × 9" (22.8 cm) long

MATERIALS

Yarn

PET BED, CAT TOY, AND DOG TOY

A worsted-weight wool and mohair yarn: total yardage required for color A: 380 yds (347 m)

A worsted-weight wool yarn: total yardage required for colors B, C, and D: 120 yds (109 m) each

Shown

Brown Sheep Lamb's Pride 85% wool / 15% mohair, worsted weight, 190 yds (174 m) / 4 oz (113 g), M100 Supreme Purple (A), 2 balls

Brown Sheep Nature Spun 100% wool, worsted weight; 245 yds (224 m) / 3.5 oz (100 g), N62 Amethyst (B), N65 Sapphire (C), 105 Bougainville (D), 1 ball each

Needles

US size 13 (9 mm) circular needle, one each 16" (41 cm) and 24" (61 cm) long

US size K/10.5 (6.5 mm) crochet hook

Notions

Tapestry needle

Scissors

Needle and thread

1 metal bell for cat toy

2 small plastic squeakers for dog toy

Gauge

8 stitches and 10 rows = 4" (10 cm) in St st

ABBREVIATIONS

LB (large bobble): (Knit, purl, knit) in next stitch. Turn work. P3 sts. Turn work. K3 sts. Turn work. P3 sts. Turn work. Knit all three stitches together.

YARN KEY

PET BED, CAT TOY, AND DOG TOY

(A) Brown Sheep Lamb's Pride Worsted – Supreme Purple

(B) Brown Sheep Nature Spun Worsted – Amethyst

(C) Brown Sheep Nature Spun Worsted – Sapphire

(D) Brown Sheep Nature Spun Worsted – Bougainville

Violet's Bed

With circular needle and one strand each of yarns A and B, CO 20 sts.

Knit 2 rows.

Increase row: K1 st, m1, knit to last st, m1, k1 st (22 sts).

Knit 1 row.

Repeat last 2 rows until 40 sts total.

Knit 50 rows.

Decrease row: K1 st, k2tog, knit to last 3 sts, k2tog, k1 st (38 sts).

Knit 1 row.

Repeat last 2 rows until 20 sts remain.

Knit 2 rows.

Pick up sts around bed base as follows: K20 sts, place marker (pm), pick up and k46 sts along first curved side, pm, pick up and k20 sts along second short side, pm, pick up and knit 46 sts along second curved side and place contrasting color marker. This marker will indicate the start and end of the rounds (132 sts). Slip all markers on each round.

Join, and k5 rnds. Cut yarn B and attach yarn C.

Decrease row: *ssk, knit to 2 st before next marker, k2tog, slip marker; rep from *, end ssk, knit to 2 sts before the last marker, k2tog, slip the last marker (124 sts).

Knit 5 rnds.

Purl 2 rnds.

* K5 sts, LB; repeat from * until 4 sts remain, k3 sts, LB.

Knit 1 rnd.

Bind off all stitches and weave in any loose strands securely.

Place pet bed in a large laundry bag, and felt according to directions on page 22.

While the bed is wet, it can be stretched to desired dimensions. Allow the bed to air dry.

○○○○○○○○○○○○○○○○○

Violet's Bed

Storm's Cat Toy

Base

With 16" (41 cm) size 13 (9 mm) circular needle and 1 strand of yarn A and 1 strand of yarn C held together as one, CO 12 sts.

Knit 2 rows.

Skp, k8 sts, k2tog (10 sts).

Knit 1 row.

Skp, k6 sts, k2tog (8 sts).

Knit 1 row.

Skp, k4 sts, k2tog (6 sts).

Knit 1 row.

Skp, k2 sts, k2tog (4 sts).

Knit 1 row.

K1 st, m1, k2 sts, m1, k1 st (6 sts).

Purl 1 row.

K1 st, m1, k4 sts, m1, k1 st (8 sts).

Purl 1 row.

K1 st, m1, k6 sts, m1, k1 st (10 sts).

Knit 1 row.

Purl 1 row.

Skp, k6 sts, k2tog (8 sts).

Purl 1 row.

Skp, k4 sts, k2tog (6 sts).

Purl 1 row.

Skp, k2 sts, k2tog (4 sts).

Purl 1 row.

K2tog across (2 sts).

K2tog (1 st).

Switch to crochet hook and ch 60.

Count 25 ch sts from hook and sl st into the next ch to form a loop.

Cut yarn and pull through loop.

Weave in any loose strands securely.

Finishing

From yarn D, cut 24 6" (15.2 cm) strands of yarn for fringe. Attach 2 strands each to the bottom 12 sts of the toy. (Directions for cutting and attaching fringe are given on page 17.)

Place the toy in a laundry bag, and felt according to directions on page 22.

While the piece is wet, it can be stretched to desired dimensions. Allow the toy to air dry, and securely sew on the metal bell using wool yarn. Make sure to check the bell periodically to ensure it does not come loose from the toy during play.

ooooooooooooooooo

Storm's Cat Toy

Simon's Dog Toy

Base

With 16" (41 cm) size 13 (9 mm) circular needle and 2 strands of yarn D held together as one, CO 6 sts.

Work 2 rows in St st.

K1 st, m1, k4 sts, m1, k1 st (8 sts).

Purl 1 row.

K1 st, m1, k6 sts, m1, k1 st (10 sts).

Purl 1 row.

K1 st, m1, k8 sts, m1, k1 st (12 sts).

Work 3 rows in St st.

Skp, k8 sts, k2tog (10 sts).

Purl 1 row.

Skp, k6 sts, k2tog (8 sts).

Purl 1 row.

Skp, k4 sts, k2tog (6 sts).

Work 17 rows in St st.

K1 sts, m1, k4 sts, m1, k1 st (8 sts).

Purl 1 row.

K1 st, m1, k6 sts, m1, k1 st (10 sts).

Purl 1 row.

K1 st, m1, k8 sts, m1, k1 st (12 sts).

Work 3 rows in St st.

Skp, k8 sts, k2tog (10 sts).

Purl 1 row.

Skp, k6 sts, k2tog (8 sts).

Purl 1 row.

Skp, k4 sts, k2tog (6 sts).

Work 3 rows in St st and bind off all stitches.

Finishing

Make one more toy base by repeating the above instructions.

With crochet hook and yarns B and C, sc the two toy bases together, starting at the middle. Leave a 3" (7.6 cm) gap open (sc only on the top base) in the middle of the toy to allow room for the squeakers.

Place the toy in a laundry bag, and felt according to directions on page 22.

Insert the two squeakers into the center opening and push them to the opposite ends of the toy. Sew the opening of the toy together securely, using scrap yarn. Make sure to check the seam periodically to ensure it does not break open during play.

ooooooooooooooo
Simon's Dog Toy

Resources

❀ All of the beautiful yarns and notions used in this book are available from the following companies. Please contact them for shops in your area.

YARN COMPANIES

Austermann
Buhlstrasse 14
D-73079 Sussen
Germany
www.austermann-wolle.de

Banwy Workshop
Llanfair Caereinion
Powys, Mid Wales SY21 0SG
United Kingdom
www.colinette.com

Berroco
P.O. Box 367
14 Elmdale Road
Uxbridge, MA 01569 USA
www.berroco.com

Brown Sheep
100662 County Road 16
Mitchell, NE 69357 USA
www.brownsheep.com

Cascade
P.O. Box 58168
Tukwila, WA 98138 USA
www.cascadeyarns.com

Cherry Tree Hill, Inc.
P.O. Box 659
Barton, VT 05822 USA
www.cherryyarn.com

Classic Elite
122 Western Ave.
Lowell, MA 01851 USA
www.classiceliteyarns.com

Colinette
Unique Kolours
28 N. Bacton Hill Rd.
Malvern, PA 19355 USA
www.uniquekolours.com

Crystal Palace Yarns

Straw into Gold

160 23rd St.

Richmond, CA 94804 USA

www.straw.com

Elann.com, Inc.

P.O. Box 18125

1215C–56th Street

Delta, BC V4L 2M4

Canada

www.elann.com

Europe Designer Yarns Ltd.

Unit 8-10 Newbridge Industrial Estate

Pitt Street, Keighley

West Yorkshire BD21 4PQ

United Kingdom

www.designeryarns.uk.com

Hemp Traders

2132 Colby Avenue, Suite #5

Los Angeles, CA 90025 USA

www.hemptraders.com

Lion Brand Yarns

34 West 15th Street

New York, NY 10011 USA

www.lionbrand.com

Noro Yarns

Knitting Fever, Inc.

P.O. Box 336

315 Bayview Avenue

Amityville, NY 11701 USA

www.knittingfever.com

Patons

P.O. Box 40

Listowel, ON N4W 3H3

Canada

www.patonsyarns.com

Plymouth Yarn Co.

Box 28

Bristol, PA 19007 USA

www.plymouthyarn.com

Schachenmayr Nomotta Coats GmbH

Kaiserstrasse 1

D-79341 Kenzingen

Germany

www.coatsgmbh.de

NOTIONS AND EXTRAS

Acid dyes:

Jacquard

www.dharmatrading.com

Glass beads:

Blue Moon Beads

www.bluemoonbeads.com

Grosgrain ribbon:

J. Caroline Creative

www.jcarolinecreative.com

Kool-Aid dyes:

Kraft Foods North America, Inc.

Box RK-WWK

Rye Brook, NY 10573 USA

www.koolaid.com

Plastic pony beads:

Create for Less

www.createforless.com

Squeakers for dog toy:

Sitstay.com

5831 North 58th Street

Lincoln, NE 68507 USA

www.sitstay.com

About the Author

Darlene Bruce has a fiber studio in her home in Charlottesville, Virginia, where she lives with her husband, Chris, and her two cats, Simon, and Storm. Specializing in natural-fiber handbags, accessories, and home décor, she sells her work at juried art and craft shows. She teaches knitting and felting classes through the University of Virginia and runs a local knitting and craft group.

Acknowledgments

Many thanks to the creative team at Rockport Publishers and Quarry Books, headed by Winnie Prentiss, who made this book possible. Special thanks to Mary Ann Hall for being a fabulous editor for this book. Thanks also to technical editor Dot Ratigan, project manager Rochelle Bourgault, and design manager Regina Grenier.

This book would not have been possible without the support of my husband, Chris. Thank you for supporting my business and giving me the freedom to write this book. You are definitely one in a million and I am a very lucky girl. I also have to thank my two cats, Simon and Storm, for providing me with lots of inspiration as I worked on the knitting patterns. Thanks especially to my cat Violet, who sadly passed away before this book was completed. She routinely slept on my lap during the many countless hours of sitting in front of the computer writing. You are such a sweet kitty.

While every effort has been made to ensure the accuracy of the knitting patterns, mistakes and typos can occur. Visit www.naturalviolet.com for the latest updates on corrections. Please also feel free to send me feedback about the book. I would love to hear from you.